Claim Your Power,

Gain Your Freedom.

Robert Rensing

To Sally Thorne,

With gratitude for
your encouragement
and support.

Robert Browning

ISBN 1. 978-0-9936200-0-3
       2. 978-0-9936200-1-0 (ebook)

ISBN-10: 0993620000

Cover Design by Linda Weech, BFA, PDPP.
www.LindaWeech.com

Disclaimer.

This book contains a description of the thoughts, dreams, perceptions, and writings of the author. It does not claim to present scientific or medical information.

The author, publishers, distributors, and sellers of this book do not accept liability of any kind in connection with the explicit or implied contents of this book.

If you require medical information, support, or treatment, we urge you contact a qualified health care practitioner.

Table of Contents.

Claim Your Power,

Gain Your Freedom.

A Journey from Conventional Thoughts

to Unconventional Dreams.

Dedication.

With His gracious permission I dedicate this book to His Holiness the XIV Dalai Lama, with gratitude for the guidance and wisdom I found in His teachings. I had the distinct honour and pleasure of meeting Him during His first visit to Vancouver, BC in April, 2004, and I cherish the memory of the brief conversation we had, when He said to me, "when your heart is full, empty your mind"; advice that I have never forgotten and have endeavoured to apply to my life and writings.

My heartfelt thanks go to Craig Matsu-Pissot, PhD. for his great editorial suggestions and his wonderful encouragement, and to "Murali" S. Muralidharan, PhD. for his expert technical knowledge and support.

I am truly grateful to Joy Larson for her unfailing encouragement and patience, and to AnneMarie Richmond, Linda Weech, Marilyn Glass, Sarah Mathison, and Tsetan Chonjore, for their many great suggestions and unfailing support.

And last but not least a big thank-you to you, my readers, for your willingness to risk stepping into a world where logic and rationality sometimes seem to be somewhat distant.

* * *

About the author.

Robert Rensing was born in the Netherlands and spent his adolescent years during the second world war German occupation of his home land. It was a troubled time and he remembers many dangers, from air raids to his Jewish neighbours being arrested in the middle of the night by German soldiers, never to be seen again.

One of his longest lasting memories was about the Dutch people celebrating allied army victories while they were sad and even angry when they suffered a defeat. Robert wondered why people would celebrate the killing of so many young women and men, and asked himself "Is there not a more humane way of settling disputes?"

That question stayed with him during his entire adult life and, after 13 years as a music conservatory principal, was the primary reason for leaving a successful second career as a human resources specialist. Instead he became a homesteader in a remote corner of the Canadian Rocky Mountains. There he finally had time to read the books he had always wanted to read, dream the dreams that were waiting for him to be experienced, and wrote poetry and short stories, a number of which have been published in various anthologies.

Then, in 1982, Robert was diagnosed with terminal bone cancer and was given 2 to 4 more weeks to live. He miraculously survived that disastrous prognosis, which in turn left him with a whole new series of questions.

These two all-too-common human challenges, mass violence and terminal cancer, are the reasons why he has written *"Claim your Power, Gain your Freedom"*. But this is much more than a self-help book. The purpose of this book is to share his experiences, insights, and the answers he gained from those. Robert hopes that you too will feel inspired to pursue innovative thinking outside the culturally sanctioned box. This *"Journey from Conventional Thoughts to Unconventional Dreams"* is about exploring how you can indeed *"Claim your Power"* and *"Gain your Freedom"*, and discover that unconventional ideas can have their feet firmly planted in daily reality and can begin to change that reality into the way you would like it to be.

* * *

Introduction.

This book starts with an allegory of a mythical man named *Wishing,* who was obsessed with the smell of freshly brewed coffee. Read it again and you may find in this story images of the universal quest for a better world - a world that has as its foundation our inborn quest for peace, happiness, wisdom, and enlightenment.

I did not invent the story of the Coffee Maker. It appeared in my mind fully developed as, in Greek mythology, the goddess Athena appeared from the forehead of Zeus fully formed and holding a symbolic spear.[1] All I had to do was to stop my ever-busy mind and start listening and writing. After finishing that, it took only minimal editing and correcting a few typos.

As heavenly as that "aroma of freshly brewed coffee" is for coffee drinkers, it is of course simply a metaphor that stands for, it seems, something that we are all born with. During the course of life it often becomes distorted or lost.

I believe that our wish for a better world is as fundamental as life itself. That belief has expressed itself in many ways, including the experience of God representing images of a perfect world. Whether you believe in God or not, it is my belief that all of us, aware of it or not, somehow "know" that there is something bigger and better than we find in daily life. It is my hope that you will rediscover the true meaning of what this metaphor represents. I am still searching for that, and I invite you to join that search.

* * *

This book presents a number of conversations between two characters that may represent archetypes. In reality these are "conversations" that manifested in my own mind over the years. The questions they pose, and the answers and insights that flowed from these, are of my own imagination, experiences, and beliefs, and the story represents how these evolved over the years.

Some topics in this book evolved slowly in my mind, and not until much later did I realize the sometimes obvious parallels to Buddhist philosophy. I make no apologies for these similarities as they developed during my process of self-discovery. Other topics, such as the concept of dependent origination, I learned directly from Buddhism and, where they are relevant to the theme of this book, I decided to include them.

* * *

Before you start reading beyond this introduction, please turn to appendix A which explains what meditation is and how to pursue its practice. Buddhism and meditation are age-old practices. They are not religious exercises and in no way interfere or compete with religious beliefs and practices. Rather, they are exercises in calming our ever-busy mind, and opening one's mind to ever-growing awareness and gaining fresh ideas, insights, and wisdom. Whether or not you are interested in meditation, I urge you to consider this practice. It is virtually indispensable to gaining benefit from the writings that follow.

It is my hope that you can stop your rational mind long enough to let this story develop a life of its own, so that you too may find your soul evolving in a direction of love, acceptance, and compassion. That gift is already present as a potential in every sentient being, waiting to develop into a fulfilling life of compassion, service, and true happiness.

We live in a world where nothing lasts – where everything will fade away after so brief a moment. You and I will soon be gone, being subject to the limited time of our existence on earth. Let us not waste our time here, there is so little of it. Let us make good use of this gift of time and dedicate ourselves to make our tiny contribution toward a better world for our children and many generations to follow.

We do have the power to work toward creating that contribution. We may or may not be successful, and what we have to offer may be miniscule. We are not expected to change the world, but we can offer something of lasting value to the next hundred generations if we start now with an open heart and mind, and practice our gift of love and compassion. Let's start now with learning the lessons for which we have come here to learn; let us make good use of our brief time here so that we may die in peace, knowing that we have not failed our children.

Beyond the world of opposites

is an unseen

but experienced

unity and identity in us all.

Joseph Campbell.

Hornby Island, BC.
September 2014.

*   *   *

Part 1.
What Happened . . ?

Prologue:

The Coffee Maker.

A Contemporary Story of the Ancient Quest for Truth.

Once upon a time, a long, long time ago, an old man was travelling through a great forest. The trees were so enormous that he couldn't even see the sky, and the light on the forest floor was so dim that he could hardly see where he was going. His name was *Wishing*.

For a long, long time Wishing felt lost in the forest. He simply could not find the end of it and so he wandered day after day. Wishing became so weary that he finally stopped and said to himself, "I just cannot find my way out. Perhaps this forest is all there is left of the world. I should stop looking for the way out, sit down and rest, and then build myself a cabin so that I have a safe place to stay."

After a long rest the old man set about to build himself a tiny cabin, but he soon realized that, to build a cabin, one needs tools: a saw, an axe, a hammer, and hinges for the door. But he had not brought any tools and so he abandoned his plans and simply had no choice but to continue to seek a way out of the great forest.

After another long time of wandering something mysterious happened: he saw a white rabbit. Wishing called to the rabbit "Please little rabbit, please stop and give me directions." The little rabbit stopped and looked long and hard at Wishing and then turned around and pointed his little pink nose due north. Wishing somehow understood what the rabbit was trying to tell him and for many days travelled due north. But the forest became darker and darker and Wishing became very fearful. Finally, he just sat down and thought, "I cannot go on any more", and closed his eyes and cried . . .

When Wishing opened his eyes again he saw the faintest of trails, almost indistinguishable. Mustering all his courage, he got up and followed the trail, and suddenly he found himself at the edge of the forest.

Wishing saw a whole big wide world before him, a world with millions of opportunities and choices. A world with the greatest undreamed-of delights. A world that beckoned him, "Come, share with me, taste my delights, find your happiness."

The old man entered this new world and came to a great city. As he wandered through its narrow streets and alleyways his nose picked up a wonderful aroma. Wishing quickened his pace, sniffing and sniffing the air and becoming more and more excited until he came to a tiny square with a small café, and from that café came the wonderful smell of fresh coffee! He stepped through the narrow doorway into the dimly lit place and, to his utter surprise, saw the most beautiful coffee maker he had ever seen. It was made of the purest gold, inlaid with sparkling precious stones, and emitting the most heavenly smell of freshly brewed coffee!

Wishing sat down and began to feel younger and younger. Not since his childhood had he smelled that wonderful coffee aroma, and during his years of wandering in the great forest he had often wished for that comforting smell to return to him even for just a moment. He ordered a cup of coffee and sat down to enjoy it, when an odd thought crept into his mind: if I drink this coffee it will soon be finished and I cannot stay here for the rest of my life waiting for a refill. I cannot bear the thought of losing this comforting smell of coffee ever again.

And so he called out to the owner of the coffee shop and said, "I cannot drink this coffee unless you give me that beautiful coffee maker, because once I taste this cup of coffee I can no longer live without it. Please give me your coffee maker".

The coffee man answered "dear friend, I have made coffee in this place for many, many years and I will continue to make more coffee until the end of my days. Making coffee is my passion and my joy, and nothing can make me happier than to fill your cup again for as long as you wish. If coffee is your passion I will honour that as long as I live, and fill your cup over and over again until you are satisfied. But I cannot give you my coffee maker because if I do I can no longer make coffee.

I cannot give you my coffee maker - I cannot give you my passion."

Wishing pleaded, "then at least please sit down for a while and share a cup with me." The coffee man answered "Yes, that I will do. Let us share all the delights of coffee and drink until we are satisfied. Come back tomorrow and together we'll enjoy coffee again. Allow me to share my passion for making coffee and please tell me about your passion for smelling the aroma of freshly brewed coffee. And when you are satisfied, go with God; become a coffee man and share these delights with those who cross your path".

The two men sat down and drank in silence, and delighted in the smell and the taste of this heavenly brew. They filled their cups again and again until they could drink no more. Then Wishing rose from his seat and addressed the coffee man, "My dearest friend, you have given me coffee to enjoy; you have given me the heavenly aroma that I have been dreaming of. You have satisfied my childhood memories and made of them a blessing in this day. I thank you and I honour you for your gift to me."

"Now I must leave. Now I will go out and find my own coffee maker, which I will treasure more than life. You have taught me that sharing my passion is the ultimate gift of love to those who will receive it."

And the old man wandered off and walked for many days until he came to a tiny village where he found a small vacant shop in a little market square. Wishing sat down and closed his eyes and prayed for a very long time. And when he opened his eyes there lay on the table before him the most precious of gold and the most luminous diamonds and rubies and sapphires, and the old man revelled in these riches. But he soon realized that again there were no tools. And he felt so disappointed; here were all the makings of the most beautiful coffee maker — and no tools to make it.

Wishing closed his eyes again and prayed fervently for the tools he needed, when a quiet voice entered his head and said, "Old man, heavenly coffee makers are not *made*. They are created in your heart. Pour your love into your passion and the coffee maker will create itself".

In that magic moment the coffee maker was created. The old man filled it with the purest of spring water and added the most aromatic coffee beans he could find in his heart. And the heavenly aroma of freshly brewed coffee wafted across the land, reaching out to all who cannot live without the aroma of freshly brewed coffee.

And in that magic moment Wishing's name was changed and he was known far and wide simply as The Coffee Maker. The old man nodded. A tear flowed from his eyes and his heart opened in boundless compassion to all who wander around in dark forests.

* * *

1. Mr. C.

Once I had a friend, a very dear friend, who was known far and wide simply as Mr. C. He was a calm and peaceful man who ran a small coffee shop in a little hole-in-the-wall in the plaza of the village where I grew up.

When I was a boy and ran into trouble, I would always go and talk with Mr. C., and it seemed that his answers to my problems were never longer than one short sentence. Once I went to him to complain that our soccer team always lost against the team from the next village. Mr. C. asked simply "But don't you like *playing* soccer?" And when I had so madly fallen in love with a beautiful girl that I could hardly sleep, he asked me "Are you really planning on marrying her?"

Not until I came back to my childhood village many years later did I realize that Mr. C. was a very wise man indeed. His clientele consisted of almost the entire village: young and old, men, women, and children, and it seemed that even the village cats and dogs tended to hang out around his modest little shop.

After I finished school I couldn't wait to go to the city, go to college, and start a career toward fame and fortune. And indeed, twenty years later I owned a large successful business, was respected by my peers for my business skills, and celebrated by one and all for my fortune, good looks, and social success. Indeed, I considered myself a success! (I even had some very beautiful girlfriends but I won't go into that just now)

And then, one day, I fainted. Nothing special, just a simple faint, caused by too much hard work, too many martinis, too much stress, too much . . . But when it happened again a few days later I went to see my doctor, who sent me to the hospital for some tests, where some other doctor ordered some X rays, where yet another doctor ordered something else, and where finally all those doctors showed up together in my room to tell me that they had some "not-so-good news".

"You have cancer"

"The prognosis is not good"

"It has spread all through your body"

"There is not much we can do for you"

"You have at best a couple of months to live"

"You better get your affairs in order"

"I don't believe it."

"They must have made a mistake"

"Oh God, if you make me better I promise that I'll quit smoking and   drinking"

"I'll kill those guys at the office who always run to me for everything"

"I guess this is for real. . . "

That was the moment when I decided to go back to my village to die among my own people. To die in peace, if I could find any of it, that is.

* * *

After I came back home I thought of Mr. C. quickly enough, but I avoided him for a long time, remembering how he had a bad habit of seeing right through me (or so it seemed). Or maybe I was secretly afraid of having anyone look through me. Maybe I was afraid that they would see something that I wasn't willing to look at just yet.

That was a new and very strange feeling. I had never been one to procrastinate. If there was a decision to be made I would make it. Now! Not later!

"And if I'm not sure about the decision I'll apply my mind to the problem and solve it."

"And I have a good brain and I make no apologies for that."

" And I know how to use good straight reasoning to solve a problem."

"So why the procrastination? I sure as hell am not afraid of anything; not even cancer!"

"So why the procrastination? What's stopping me? What 's going on?"

That's when I decided that I'd better pay Mr. C. a visit.

* * *

I've always loved coffee. I remember when I was just a kid that I would stand outside his coffee shop and just inhale that wonderful aroma of freshly brewed coffee. Of course, when I grew up I drank gallons of the stuff at the office, but most of it was pretty toxic and, although it didn't give me ulcers, it was a habit more than real enjoyment.

When I walked up to Mr. C's little shop all those childhood memories came surging back again and I just stood there for several minutes, enjoying that heavenly aroma.

When I entered the shop everything changed very quickly. Mr. C. said hello and then just looked at me. He didn't even ask how I was; he just looked and it felt as if I was 5 years old again and Mr. C. was just looking through me. Something was happening to this hard-nosed business man — the man with the good brain and no fear of decision making. To tell you the truth, I didn't like it one bit . . .

And then he said, "How about a cup of good coffee?", and I relaxed and felt at home again.

We didn't talk about anything in particular that morning. He asked me how life in the city was for me, and how my business was going, and if last winter had been as cold in the city as it had been in the village. And I told him that things were going alright, and that I had not been feeling too well lately, (probably too much hard work and stress) but that I expected that it would all blow over soon. And when I had finished my coffee I just thanked him and left.

So what was the big deal about going for a coffee at Mr. C's?

* * *

I came back several times after that first visit. We just sat quietly and enjoyed our coffee. But it wasn't long until questions started popping up in my mind. At first I resisted them as I really didn't want to spoil our peace and quiet. It had been a long time since I sat with someone I care for without having to talk all the time. But the questions and my ever-busy mind just wouldn't let up.

I told Mr. C. my story in dribs and drabs, as much as I could more or less comfortably tell. He never asked any questions at all, which at first upset me greatly until I got used to it. It wasn't that he was not interested. It just seemed that he took everything I said at face value. Until one day, many coffees later, he asked just one question, "Why did you do the things you did?".

I didn't have to search far for an answer, "Because this is the way life is. You do your best, you work as hard as you can and, if luck is with you, you succeed."

Mr. C. just smiled. "So you have no choice in the matter?"

"Yes, of course I do. I make the best decisions I can, work as hard as I can, and don't lose track of my goals."

"So, if you do have choices you can make, then why did you make the ones you did?"

"Oh, come on now, you cannot go through life without making choices!"

"Indeed you cannot. But my question was, why did you make the choices you made. Why did you not choose another path? "

"Well, ultimately it doesn't matter. In the end you still end up in the same place. Like that famous saying, "without human beings this would be a perfect world!" And you know what? This isn't a perfect place!"

"Well, could you make it a perfect world — could you not make your *own* world perfect?"

"Oh, come on, Mr. C., don't ask silly questions!"

"Oh my friend, haven't you seen the beauty around you? Haven't you breathed the fresh air? Haven't you seen the sun rise? Haven't you heard the birds sing in springtime? Haven't you ever loved life just for its own sake?"

"Maybe I have, but I also have to make a living and that is a world that is not beautiful at all. It's competitive and harsh and dog-eat-dog! That is the real world I have to live in and survive in. There is nothing beautiful in that at all. And then, when you finally find yourself a winner, the roof caves in and cancer makes its grand entrée. You call that beauty!? You know, even without human beings around, this still wouldn't be a perfect world. Songbirds are won-derful until they get caught and eaten by a hawk. Sunsets are beautiful until it rains. So what about that beauty?"

Mr. C. just sat there and smiled, "Would you like to find out?"

I got up and left.

* * *

I did a lot of very confused thinking that night. I respect Mr. C. enough to know that he was trying to tell me something important. But I also have 40 years of real life experience that tells me that beauty is a wonderful idea that doesn't stand up to real life.

Do I want to see beauty? Yeah, of course I do. Do I think that beauty is a part of every-day life? NO!

But what is Mr. C. trying to tell me? I don't think he is trying to give me a hard time just for the fun of it. What does he want from me? Why is he pushing me to where I don't want to go? I already have enough on my plate with that damn cancer. Why the hell doesn't he just shut up and leave me alone!

With that I became wound up enough to give up on trying to sleep. I got up again and went for a long walk instead.

Anger has never played a big part in my life. If there is something I don't like or someone makes a stupid mistake I'll just tell him so and get it out of the way. That's not being angry, that's being honest and up-front. And everybody sure knows where I stand at all times. Yeah, and that's not "beauty" either – just survival skills.

The next morning I didn't go for coffee with Mr. C. Nor the next day. And I felt lost and disoriented. But don't bug me with that "life is beautiful" crap!

* * *

You know, anger is a strange thing. It is powerful enough all right, and it hides behind justifications and rationalizations. But what it really is I still don't know. In retrospect it seems that I needed that cancer to rub my nose into it hard enough so that I would finally begin to pay attention. Was that the purpose of my cancer?

Hey, hey, hold it. Who is talking about a purpose in cancer? For that matter, wouldn't a purpose in cancer imply that there is "someone" who is giving it to me because "it's good for me"?

When I asked Mr. C. about this thought a few weeks later he gave a, for him, rather long speech. He said, "I don't believe that anything of any importance just happens by blind coincidence. Hawks catch and eat song birds because hawks have to eat. Too bad for the little song bird, but that is how physical life works. Sunrises happen daily because the earth rotates – if it didn't the earth would long ago have been swallowed up by the enormous gravity forces of the sun. Etcetera, etcetera."

The next day Mr. C. continued, "Now, about cancer: you don't get cancer by blind coincidence; you don't get cancer by the luck of the draw; you don't get cancer as "punishment" for your "sins". If that were true we would all have cancer by now. So why do you have cancer? As always, there are two kinds of 'why'. The first can be "what caused my cancer to happen, in a physical sense?"

- Poor lifestyle
- Bad diet
- Lack of exercise

- Smoking
- Alcohol / drug abuse
- Genetic predisposition
- Some viruses
- Environmental toxins
- Stress
- Depression
- Long-term negative emotions

And usually a combination of several of these plus many others. However I know a number of people who smoke like chimneys but never get lung cancer. And I know quite a few others who have never smoked but did get lung cancer anyway. Figure that out . . .

All persons have cancerous cells in their bodies during much of their lives but normally one's immune system takes care of them. But under certain circumstances the immune cells may be unable to keep things under control and allow cancerous cells to multiply uncontrolled.   This is essentially what cancer is."

* * *

At this point I had heard about as much as I could handle.

"Why are you telling me all this?"
"Are you telling me all about what I have been doing wrong in my life?"

"Are you trying to sell me a king-size guilt trip?"

Mr. C. answered simply, "I'm afraid you'll have to seek your own answers to these questions. All I have told you about is a bit about the "mechanics" of cancer and a bit about the "you" that you know. When you're ready we'll talk about the part of you that you don't know."

I could feel my blood coming to a boil again and I could barely keep my anger under control; I had just about heard enough and left in a not very good mood.

* * *

It took me several days to cool down, especially because there seemed to be something nagging me in the back of my mind, something that I couldn't quite put my finger on but that continued to bug me. At one point it made me angry all over again, until I began to realize that 'it' couldn't care less about my being angry.

Perhaps it was anger itself that was bugging me?

Is there something going on in myself that I hardly even know about?

Is that what Mr. C is talking about?

But cancer is caused by something — couldn't possibly be by some angry thoughts.

Well, I better go and see what Mr. C. has to say about that . .

* * *

The next morning I was off for a cup of coffee again at Mr. C's. He continued, "As I mentioned the other day, there is a second 'why' in that question about why you have cancer, that is of an entirely different nature. Change the question from "*Why* did I get cancer" to "Why did *I* get cancer" and it becomes an completely different question.

"While that first question is an external one: what happened to me, what did I do (or not do) that caused me to have cancer. The second question is one that has to do with "I", with "me". It is an "internal" question that applies to what is happening inside of me, not *"What* is it that I have been avoiding in my life" but "*Why* have I been avoiding things in my life to the point where I need my nose rubbed into it?"

"What is it in me that I need to change?"
"What is it in me that I need to learn?"

In the context of this second why, the world around us plays only a secondary role. The focus is on me. What is it in me that I need to change or learn?

Of course you could ask another question now: what makes you think that there is anything that requires changing in life? Because if it were true that I need to change and learn, I cannot escape the idea that there must be some sort of purpose in life.

Hey, isn't that going a bit far. . . ?

* * *

I felt strangely subdued after our conversation. It seemed that my cancer is playing some secret role in all that. But if nothing else, the cancer seems to act as a wake-up call and tries to pry my mind open to new ideas and broader perspectives.

And all of a sudden I realized that this time I did not get angry, a first for me! I don't like to be questioned or challenged, and yet that seems to be exactly what Mr. C. is doing. With, until today, some predictable result. I'd be totally pissed off and angry at . . .

At what?
My cancer?
Myself?
Life?
Fate?

Isn't the purpose of life to be successful?
To win,
To get to the top,
To gain other people's respect and admiration.
Did I really waste that much of my life with things that are not the purpose of life?

So why do I feel so strangely subdued? Why don't I get angry and get on with things rather than waste my time with some philosophical questions and ideas?

Just a minute, what's going on here?

* * *

The next morning I was back at Mr. C's again.

"So what do you think is the purpose in my life, Mr. C.?"

"Before we get into that, tell me, how do you feel right now?"

"I don't know. Rather strange and subdued. I'm not sure how to describe it."

"Well, it seems that something is working inside you, a new and, to you, somewhat strange process. I don't want to interfere with that. Better to let it run its own course. So for now I'll pass and let you think a bit more about what your purpose in your life might be. Stick with those thoughts and you'll find answers beginning to show up in your mind."

"Don't try and analyze those thoughts and answers. They are part of a process that takes time to develop. Just listen to what shows up, respect it and, if you cannot make head or tail of it, just let it be. It will become clearer to you over time."

And with that advice, he got us a big cup of coffee and talked about simple things. Apparently he had said what he needed to say and the rest is up to me.

* * *

Once an idea or thought enters my mind I stick with it, I pursue it, I investigate it, I won't let go till I understand it and know all the ins and outs. Some people have called it obsessive. I call it stubborn inquisitiveness.

Ideas are there to tell me something. Sometimes it just tells me what to do or where to go. Call it intuition and, as irrational as intuition seems to be, it has been a cornerstone of my success in life, and many good business decisions have been based on that. But sometimes those ideas have nothing to do with practical stuff. They seem to indicate a train of thought that sometimes develops very slowly but always leads to new insights and understandings. Mr. C's remarks sparked one of those ideas.

* * *

2. Life [is] like a shadow with a broken roof, With stars shining through its holes.[2]

I had a very strange dream last night. I dreamed that I was walking in a strange city, wearing bright purple sunglasses with warped lenses. All the colours were weird and my sight was totally distorted. I felt very strange and disoriented, so I tried to take my glasses off but it was impossible to remove them. It was as if they were welded onto my nose. I continued to wander around until I couldn't even remember where I was heading.

This morning I told Mr. C about my dream. He just grinned and said, "So, you were looking through coloured distorting glasses and couldn't remember your goal? Could you remember where you were going when you first started out? Who originally put those glasses on your nose?"

I didn't have the faintest idea of what he was talking about so I just finished my coffee and headed back home. But the dream kept bothering me and so, after lunch, I laid down for a brief nap. But of course I started thinking again: Where did those glasses come from, who put them there, and why couldn't I take them off? I couldn't make head or tail of it and pretty soon I drifted off to sleep.

. . . And had another dream: I was working in a shoe store. In the stockroom there were shelves full of shoe boxes, each with one pair of shoes in them, every pair different, but all boxes the same. A customer had asked me for a particular pair of shoes and I started reading all the labels to find the right kind. But all the labels just read "shoes". It was maddening and there was nothing I could do other than tell the customer that all the boxes were the same. My customer just looked at me and said, "Then why are you working in a shoe store?"

I woke up suddenly, upset by that darn shoe store dream and too restless to go back to sleep. So I got up, straightened my clothes and went for a walk to air out my brain.

And then, all of a sudden, it dawned on me: Here I am working in a shoe store or whatever and all the labels are the same. Nothing says any-thing different. Have I spent a whole life working, never doing anything different except making more money, being more successful, and exchanging one beautiful girlfriend for another one? Has anything ever changed in my life since I went to the big city, except that I continued to feel more power-ful, more important and more successful? Is that all there is to life? That walk to air out my mind lasted for many hours!

* * *

The next morning when I went for coffee to Mr. C's he asked me "Why did you never marry? A good looking man like you should be able to find a wonderful caring wife!"

The answer was not far away. Why should I bother with all the time, attention and energy it takes to make a marriage work? After all, I've had numerous very good-looking girlfriends with whom I shared some very good times. But the question made me think: what is marriage all about and how does one go about finding the "right" woman? It all sounds so easy; find someone with whom you can have great sex and if everything is working well, why not get married?

But if it is that easy, why do 50% of all marriages fail? Surely the people involved didn't start out on some ill-intended adventure? Or did they after all?

It finally dawned on me that sexual attraction is only a very small part of the whole picture. I well remember my own childhood: a remote father who seldom really talked with me, a mother who was so self-occupied that she didn't have a lot of time to read or play with me and who was ever ready to criticize my smallest fault. So I grew up learning very quickly that being "self-contained" was the safest place to be. This never entered my mind when I met a new girlfriend. Sex was uppermost in my mind and all that psychological stuff was of no interest to me.

But if we would actually get married, how long would this euphoria last? How long until I again became self-sufficient and self-contained, and retreat into the safe space of my work and find my marriage fizzle out? How long could a partner or wife put up with me and with her own hidden fears and shortcomings, whether real or imagined? Maybe I should go easy on the sex and spend a lot more time getting to know myself a lot better, and ditto for my girl friend,

But why am I so intent on being self-sufficient? As asked myself that question, long-forgotten memories started to pop up again. Sometimes these are just little things, like walking down a street and all-of-a-sudden seeing a person who looks awfully familiar without being able to place him. Only later would I remember that he reminded me of a neighbour of 25 years ago or something like that.

But sometimes these long-forgotten memories influence very important events, for example a beautiful new girlfriend. Great, but don't lose my independence.

The old and forgotten memory that triggers that response? Remote parents = look after myself and remain self-sufficiently independent; have a good time but don't let it become serious and don't let things develop beyond a nice adventure.

And the hidden fears that come with this: getting married? No way, I'm not getting too close and then find that I have become an uninvited appendix to someone else's life. I'd sooner get back to my business again and maybe find another (temporary) girlfriend later. Perhaps this explains how I became a successful businessman bachelor . . ?

* * *

3. And Then the Roof Caved In.

What happened next was of a very differ-ent nature; I got a phone call from the hospital this morning, telling me to be there tonight at 4 o'clock as my surgery was scheduled for the next morning.

I made it as far as the reception desk, where I was told to sit in a wheelchair because, if I would fall, the hospital could be liable. Not a good start. So I was wheeled to my room, told to strip and put on a hospital gown, and wait. Supper was terrible and I was nervous and afraid.

After supper I walked down the corridor to a solarium. There was nobody there so I closed the door and sat down, looking through a large pic-ture window at a park. I don't know how long I sat there when I got the feeling that someone else had entered the room. I remember looking back over my shoulder but there was nobody there.

That feeling of someone being there persisted. It felt as if somebody was standing behind me, just behind my right shoulder, but I paid no further atten-tion to it. I felt pretty upset and angry by the whole course of events, but after I while I became aware that, quite unexpectedly, I had become totally calm and peaceful.

I must have sat there for a very long time. Gradually that sense of "presence" faded, and I returned to my room. The last thing I remember was telling the nurse that I felt fine and didn't need a sleeping pill.

* * *

The next morning no breakfast of course, and after a while a nurse came and gave me a shot of sedative to make me feel relaxed. And then, just as my mind was beginning to relax, I unexpectedly realized again that I was dying. The doctors had told me that there was no hope for my recovery and that the surgery was just to reduce the pain and make me more comfortable for whatever time I had left. That thought, which I had carefully avoided so far, at first shocked me. But after a while it became almost comfortable; there was nothing I could do about it. I was dying and that was the end of it.

The end of what? That became a big question in my mind. Before this moment I had "known" that everybody sooner or later will die, but I had given little thought to what that really meant. Now I was facing the music full force. Dying what? Would there be anything left of me (other than my dead body)? Would anything of me survive? If so, what kind of judgment would I have to face? How would I explain or justify all the mistakes I had made in my life, all the people I had intentionally or unintentionally hurt? I was in turmoil, worried sick about what lay ahead and frantically looking for a way out. But I was dying, and there was no way out.

Or was there? Who had convinced me that there would be a terrible judgment ahead? Who had told me that when you are dead it is "game over"? Who had planted these fears in my mind? That was the kind of argument that was raging in my mind.

And then something mysterious happened. My mind just quit. I was no longer thinking, I was just lying there in bed, wondering what I was going to do after my body died, and a great feeling of peace and acceptance washed over me like a huge wave. I was OK after all!

That was about the last thing I can remember. Hardly any recollection of the surgery although I had the impression that I heard one doctor comment "Boy, look at that", presumably about something they found inside my body, although I'm not sure that I actually heard it. But I do remember coming to in the recovery room and, after the fog lifted a bit, I remember thinking, "So this is what it is like when you are dead".

But I wasn't. In fact I was very much alive, and my mind almost immediately went back to where it was at before I went into the surgery. So there is no judgment, so there is nothing to fear, so death isn't a big deal. My mind became totally clear and translucent, like a clear blue sky. Not a cloud to be seen.

I was floating, I was totally present. No thoughts of the past any more, no worries about the future that wasn't here yet anyway. Just present. I became vividly aware that "something" had changed in me; I am OK just the way I am. Yes, there are several things I would like to change in my thoughts and behaviours, but I am OK just the way I am.

What would I like to change? I would very much like to see the people around me as just human beings who are struggling to make sense out of their life; who are struggling with their own little issues and old hidden memories but are too busy to really pay attention to those around them. Who find their problems so big that they don't know how to cope with them and so just avoid them. Who are so busy keeping themselves under control that they can only respond to those around them with selfishness, aggression, and self-importance. Who are so unsure about themselves that they have to present themselves just a little bigger and better and more impor- tant than they really are.

Of course I was really only talking about myself, the "myself" that I wasn't very proud of anymore but didn't know what to do with. But also, it was about the "myself" that was my past, and there was nothing that commanded me to keep going back there all the time. All I could do was to be present and stay in the present as it slowly pro- ceeds like a movie on a screen, one frame at the time.

I felt like I was being liberated from myself: nothing I must do. Just lie in bed, get better, and stay within myself getting used to the fact that there is nothing expected of me, not by myself, not by anyone else. For the first time in my life I felt truly FREE !   (cf. Appendix B)

* * *

I spent an entire week in the hospital before they let me go home. One more remarkable thing happened during that week. In the afternoon of the third day after my surgery three doctors showed up in my room: my family doctor, the surgeon, and a young intern. They of course did the usual prodding and poking but they were remarkably uncommunicative. I finally told them that I would really like to know the results of the surgery, whereupon the surgeon said, "I am not really sure"! Somewhat taken aback I mumbled something like, "Well, you out of all people should know". He then told me something that really confused me: before the surgery they had of course done a biopsy which confirmed that I had indeed cancer. After the surgery the tumour that they had removed was sent to the lab, and the lab results showed it was *not* cancerous. Everything was checked and double-checked to make sure that no mistakes were made or samples mixed up. Nothing of the sort was found. Subsequent CT scans confirmed that my brain and liver metastases had also disappeared.

So did I have cancer or did I not? The surgeon said quite correctly, "I am not really sure." My doctor and the surgeon looked rather confused; the young intern just nodded at me and smiled. Intuitively I do know. That indefinable presence in the solarium that stood behind me the evening before the surgery surely had something to do with it. Don't ask me anything specific — I don't know. But the remarkable thing was that my feelings at that time changed from anger and fear to calm and peace. Proof? No, of course not, but for me it is clear enough: I was not yet finished with my life and ready to die; I still had lessons to learn.

And this is where my real story begins.

* * *

4. Trying to make sense out of . . . what?

The journey I embarked on was energized by two experiences: one of course was the mysterious disappearance of cancer; the second was my experience when I woke up from the anaesthetic: *"I felt like I was being liberated from myself: nothing I must do. Just lay there in bed, get better, and stay within myself, getting used to the fact that there is nothing expected of me – not by myself, not by anyone else. For the first time in my life I felt truly FREE !"*

I was diagnosed with osteosarcoma (bone cancer). The primary tumour, the size of a large marble, was located on my lower jaw, and some people had commented that I looked like a chipmunk with one very full cheek. The cancer had metastasized (spread) to secondary tumours on my brain and liver. It was the primary tumour that was removed during surgery.

Over the 30 years since that surgery I have been free and clear of all cancer despite the fact that several doctors had declared my cancer to be "terminal".

But why did the tumour that was removed turn out to be not malignant? I have already described the curious sensation that "someone" stood behind

my right shoulder while I was sitting in that hospital solarium the night before the surgery, and various people have asked me, "Who was it?" Frankly,
it never occurred to me to ask that question during that experience. Was it God (by whatever name
you know It), was it Jesus, or Mohammed, or the
Buddha, or the spirit of one of my ancestors? I don't
know, and it seems rather unimportant to ascribe
this event to a particular entity. It simply happened.

I have no doubt that this experience contributed
to my miraculous healing. I don't know how or why,
but it happened and changed my life in a fundamental way. Not in an immediate or dramatic way, but
it sent me on a path that I continue to travel to this
day and surely will for the rest of my life. It made
me look inside myself for the reasons why I ended
up with terminal cancer and what I can do to make
sure that it never happens again.

It took, quite literally, a few years to get back
on my emotional feet. I was greatly exercised (such
a nice old-fashioned term but it describes exactly
how I felt) by thoughts about why I survived cancer
against almost insurmountable odds. The doctors
had after all given me not much more than a few
weeks left to live, and here I am in perfect health
30 years later. It was a puzzle that I couldn't figure
out.

Initially I felt thoroughly confused and wondered
whether this was all real. Did I start to imagine
things? I was very confused, afraid, and angry by the
time I ended up in the hospital. Was that "visit" in

the hospital solarium just imagination, if not hallu-cination? But I did know very clearly that the doctors told me before the surgery that I had bone cancer.

But then all of a sudden I didn't. Somebody must have made a mistake somewhere. Maybe someone in the lab where they test these things had not paid attention and mixed up the samples. Maybe the apparatus they use to check biopsy samples malfunctioned. Or someone misread the results. Or maybe. . .

When I couldn't make head or tail of all this, my thinking changed. Maybe the doctors didn't want to get me too depressed with bad news so they told me that there was some doubt about the nature of the tumour. But if that were true, how come I am still healthy now, rather than have relapsed into illness?

Later I thought that perhaps I was "chosen" for some special task, but I can think of a lot of people who would be much better qualified to perform such "special tasks" than I am, so that thought didn't make much sense either.

Do I perhaps still have a "lesson" to learn in this life? But doesn't everybody else have life lessons to learn also? Perhaps I am already so far advanced on my path that I should have an opportunity to finish my "studies" before I die? Well, just take one quick look at my life so far and you'll discover immedi-ately that this doesn't apply to me even remotely. I could not think of any reason why I should not be

dead (to put it bluntly). It made no sense whatso-
ever . . .

All this confusion and doubting lasted for a very
long time, but eventually my mind probably just
gave up trying to make sense out of a non-rational
experience. I remember thinking at some point in
time "this makes no sense, there is no rhyme or reason in this whole affair". And that thought evolved
into: if there is no rhyme or reason in this, why do
I keep looking for a rational explanation for something that isn't rational? Perhaps life isn't as linearly
logical as it is supposed to be. Let's start thinking in
terms of "sometimes things simply happen because
they do", as in imagination and dreams.

This is where I made my first shift in consciousness; it simply depends on how wide I am willing
to open the doors of my mind to new thoughts and
ideas, rather than remain stuck in a conventional
way of trying to find answers to unanswerable
questions.

* * *

The famous Swiss philosopher and psychiatrist
Carl Jung believed that human beings are fundamentally "whole", but most of us have lost touch
with important parts of ourselves. Through listening
to the messages of our dreams and of our creative
imagination, we can reach the lost or neglected
parts of ourselves and reintegrate them. This inte-
gration Jung understood to be the goal of life. He
called it "individuation": the process of coming

to know and accept *all* the parts of oneself, and learning to give them harmonious expression. Jung saw each human being as having a specific nature and calling, which is uniquely his or her own, and unless these are recognized and fulfilled through a union of the conscious and the unconscious, the individual can become dysfunctional and feel mentally unwell. [3]

That suited my trait of fierce independence well: become my own person, make my own decisions, be the centre of my own universe. But then doubts began to creep in again. If I am at the centre of my own universe, and you are the centre of yours, how many universes are there? And if there is only one universe (as must be obvious), how many persons can be at the centre of that one universe? Does this suggest an "inner universe"? But in that case, does it matter if I am at the centre or off-centre of my own personal universe?

More thinking, more confusion. It just wouldn't add up properly. There must be something fundamentally wrong with my train of thought. Perhaps seeing persons as individuals is an invalid concept, although our (Western) society seems to be firmly married to that idea. Are there alternative ways of perceiving human beings?

I began to think that there must be indeed other ways of perceiving ourselves. That started with a totally innocuous event: one day many years ago I turned on the radio and it happened to be playing Frank Sinatra's wonderful song "Fly me to the

Moon". Somehow my mind jumped to, "What a dream; how romantic can you get; how far away is this from everyday reality?" Or is it this "everyday reality" that is the dream? We don't live in a world that is exactly overflowing with happiness. What is real? Are we, as human beings, real? Where have we gone off the tracks?

`   Carl Jung once said, "Who looks outside, dreams; who looks inside, awakes."

Maybe it's time to pay Mr. C. a visit again . . .

*   *   *

5. Dependent Arising.

I went to see Mr. C. again at his modest little coffee shop. He was there of course, as always.

"Good to see you again, my friend. How are you feeling?"

"Well, I feel much better although I will need a little time to catch up with myself. But thank heavens that surgery and everything is over and done with." And I proceeded to tell him everything about my hospital adventure, including about that strange "visit" in the solarium and about that feeling of freedom after I woke up from the anaesthetic.

Mr. C. did not seem very surprised. "It sounds like you are ready to start on another adventure . . . I'm not too surprised about your feeling of finding freedom. That kind of insight, I like to call it wisdom, has always been present in your life, but for some reason you have kept it out of sight, stored away in your subconscious mind. Anaesthetic sometimes helps to bring that sort of insights to the foreground, but remember that anaesthetic and other drugs only let you peek behind a curtain. A glimpse is not a true experience, so let me know when you feel ready to start your new adventure and we can talk a bit about it".

* * *

The next time I visited Mr. C he presented me with an interesting concept: In Buddhism there is a fundamental principle called "dependent arising" (sometimes called "dependent origination"). It states that all phenomena, whether material or non-material, do not originate and exist independently, that is, in their own right or under their own power. Rather, their existence depends entirely on the parts that they are made of, where the phenomenon came from, and where it is going. Those parts included matter from the smallest sub-atomic particles to the largest objects, as well as all forms of energy, thoughts and emotions.[4]

As simple as this may seem at first sight, this principle produces important consequences. Let's take this chair as a brief example of what this means. This chair is here; I can see it, I can touch it, and I sit on it. And since there is no doubt about my vision, that object is present and looks like a chair. But what is it really?

One day there was a beautiful tree in a forest. Then a man came along and cut it down, cut off the branches, and cut the trunk into sections. The driver of a logging truck transported those to a saw mill where they were cut into lumber. The lumber was kiln-dried and transported to a furniture factory.

Meanwhile, a worker in a paint factory was making varnish by mixing various components together. Some of it was transported to the same furniture factory. Ore from an iron mine was shipped to a foundry where it was melted down and transformed into steel, which was shaped into nails and bolts, which were shipped to that same furniture factory as well.

At the same time a furniture designer was thinking about how to make a really sturdy and interesting looking chair. It took quite a bit of drawing to come up with a good design, but he eventually succeeded and sent his plans to the production floor where all the components were manufactured and assembled into the beautiful chair on which I am now sitting.

Of course, over the years the finish will wear off, there will be dents and scratches in the wood, and the chair will start creaking. Eventually I will have to buy a new chair and will probably cut the old one into fire wood, which will provide some much needed heat in our cold winters. The wood will turn into ashes which I will put on my garden next spring so that it will grow beautiful onions and carrots. Think of all the many steps it took for the tree to become a chair, and eventually change into onions and carrots.

Is the chair real? Yes, but only temporarily and in complete dependence on all those materials and processes it went through to become a chair: physical work, energy to run the machines, mental processes to design the chair and operate the machinery, and value judgments to make it sturdy and beautiful. Obviously, the chair did not materialize out of thin air; it does not exist in its own right and is entirely dependent on all the materials and processes that brought it into existence, only to eventually become onions and carrots: dependent arising. Dependent arising means exactly *that*: everything is part of a never-ending process, and nothing exists in its own right. Everything depends on matter and energy such as electricity, thoughts, emotions, and life itself (if that designer had not been alive, he could not have designed the chair!). *In*dependent arising does not exist. It cannot exist because there are no objects, thoughts, values, or energies that exist entirely separately from everything else, i.e. without having arisen from, and evolved into something else. (We'll come back to this in Chapter 10.)

Are you wondering about the dependent arising of thoughts and emotions? Can thoughts and emotions exist without a brain (yours or someone else's)? Are they not the result of experiences? I cannot be angry unless there is something to be angry about; I cannot think about the weather or life unless the weather and life already exist, regardless of whether or not we are consciously aware of them or not.

What does this all mean in daily life? We already know that things don't just appear out of thin air. We know that trees don't just change into carrots and onions. We already know that change requires a process to take place. The message is that everything is just temporary and will continue to change forever.

Perhaps looking at this principle again with new eyes will remind us not to become too attached to our material possessions, a good thing to pay attention to in this materialistic world. We would do well to ask ourselves what is of real lasting value and not as transitory as a new car, the latest political issue, the next TV program or sports game, or the exciting new girl friend.

* * *

The next day, over a fresh cup of coffee, Mr. C. continued: why am I telling you this example of a tree that will ultimately become an onion? Because, as I said yesterday, the concept of dependent arising presents important consequences:

1. Awareness can produce change.

The term "sentient beings" is originally a Buddhist term. It signifies conscious awareness of and beyond oneself. Sentience is the essential quality that distinguishes living beings from machines. When you think back to Wishing's wandering in the dark forest, you will realize that Wishing was aware of the fact that he was lost in a dark forest, which motivated him to get out. An un-aware animal would adopt the forest as it's reality and make it his home.

2. A change in any one component will alter the "end product".

The most obvious consequence is that everything depends entirely on its processes and components for its existence and cannot exist without that dependence. In Wishing's case he changed from being a lost wanderer, through a number of life-changing experiences into a wise old man. With his increasing awareness, his willingness to open his mind to what the owner of the coffee shop shared with him, and his ability to finally give up his attempts to control his situation, he became the "knowing" old man: "The Coffee Maker"

3. Awareness produces knowledge, which is required for making conscious choices.

Some animals may have limited ability to make conscious choices. When my dog Macks runs after something and I call him back, he often pointedly ignores me (selective listening?). But after a bit he stops and looks back with a questioning look. He knows darn well that he should come back when I call him, but he chose to ignore me, at least temporarily. On the other hand, a rabbit runs off at full speed when I try to call it and the choice is made instinctively, and not based on conscious observation and choice.

With knowledge and awareness, a person may decide to turn around or run away. One observes, makes choices based on information collected, and makes decisions based on that information and on insight and understanding gained from previous experiences. If one cannot see any reasons for turning either way one may become unsure and perhaps worry whether one made the right choice. Such is our need for knowledge in order to make a choice.

4. Knowledge can be factual and/or intuitive.

What about Wishing's white rabbit? Perhaps Wishing had a brief snooze and was only dreaming about a white rabbit. But whether he was dreaming or the rabbit was real, he decided to trust what he observed: the rabbit was pointing its nose due north and Wishing decided that he had to go in that direction to find his way out of the forest. Of course he could also have decided to shoot the rabbit and have a wonderful rabbit stew for dinner that night. There were choices.

Wishing's next choice somehow was to leave the little shop after the owner would not give him his coffee maker. Wishing could also have stayed around and come back for coffee every morning for the rest of his life, a comfortable routine for an older man! But he chose to hit the road without knowing where he was going or what to expect.

5. Trust and control have an inverse relationship; the more you trust, the less you need to control.

Next he entered the empty little shop in another village and finally let go of control. And lo and behold, the materials for a coffee maker appeared out of nowhere.

6. Unconditional love and compassion need to be learned through experiencing life with a deep awareness.

More prayer, insight, intentional living: "Pour your love into your passion . . ." and the coffee maker was magically created. Mr. C., as he is now known, stayed there and became the wise and compassionate hermit of his village. He made some very wise choices but had to give up control to get that far.

7. Liberation

We all have the potential for these qualities but they need to be developed to become fully functional. When that is reached we have become free of (that is, no longer controlled by) all the negatives that are part of our personal life. That's called Liberation.

Of course these are all metaphors.

They are also life!

Is life a metaphor?

Of what?

6. A Lecture and More Question.

During our conversation the next morning Mr. C. made a rather sweeping statement: "before we continue our conversations there is something else that I want to share with you. Life on earth essentially consists of two "layers": plant life and animal life (from single-cell life forms to whales). Yes, I know that there may be other forms of life, for example there are certain micro-organisms that can live in environments that are devoid of oxygen, that live in places where the environment consists of water and sulphuric acid. But for the present we'll limit ourselves to plant and animal life: animal life that includes microbes, fish, insects, reptiles, birds, mammals (and yes, even humans) and so many others."

Plant life depends directly on sun light, water, and minerals. Without the sun there would be virtually no plant life on earth. Plants, through the mechanism of photosynthesis, uses the energy of the sun to convert carbon dioxide into sugars (stored in carbohydrate molecules), and produces free oxygen.

Animal life can be divided into herbivores that obtain their energy from plants by converting leaves, fruit, roots, etc. into proteins; and carnivores that feed on herbivores to obtain the proteins they need. Carnivores higher on the food chain feed on the "lower" carnivores. Omnivores bridge these two categories.

This leads to untold physical suffering. Just imagine what a penguin experiences when it is caught by a seal; or what a seal experiences when it is caught by a great white shark off the coast of South Africa. Or, closer to home, how a mouse feels when it is caught by your cat. In this physical world suffering is unavoidable: the result of the principle that every form of life needs to obtain energy in order to continue living. And they get it wherever they can, even if it includes stealing it (eating) from other living beings.

The following are the fundamental instinctual drives that energize the never-ending competition between and within species:

☐ survival   - eat and be eaten,
☐ reproduction - the continuation of the species;
☐ power   - social and gender dominance,
☐ competition - between individuals, clans, and tribes for territory and resources.

That is the environment that we humans have evolved from or, for our creationist friends, how God created us human beings with instinctual drives that are similar to the ones we can observe in the animal world. The competition for energy, procreation, power, dominance, territory, and resources, still very much drive our daily behaviours

As science demonstrates, chimpanzees are our closest "relatives". There are species with which we share many genetic traits. But these nice chimps also have some not-so-nice traits: they form raiding parties which enter the territory of other chimp clans, attack them, kill some of them, and eat their victims: cannibalism! Sounds eerily like human behaviour although we no longer eat our victims. But until quite recently cannibalism was still practised by some remote tribes in New Guinea.

In many ways we have evolved well beyond the average animal state, but humanity is still subject to the never-ending quest for

- energy (food and water, and fossil fuel),
- safety (don't get "eaten" by a lion, a speeding car, a virus, or poisonous chemicals),
- security (avoid being attacked verbally, physically, or emotionally through accident, war and terrorists),
- dominance (whether by bullies or corporate CEO's) and
- the resulting competition (whether "marketing" or sports games). Here is the principle of Dependent Origination again: change one component and it will directly or indirectly change an entire culture, from individuals to an entire society.

In addition we also have to try and deal with the aftermath of traumas, both their immediate impact, and the resulting emotional charge, which often goes "underground" into the subconscious mind if it has not been effectively dealt with. Are we really "in control" of our own individuated lives, or are we being driven by age-old drives and instincts that we often are only dimly aware of?

This was essentially the end of Mr. C's lecture, and with this rather unhappy question I left for home, trying to come to terms with a picture of a world that seems a total mess. I could not help but wonder if it is evolution that has led us into this mess of a world we live in.

Mr. C's lecture left me full of doubts and questions. Is our present world environment really the best humanity has been able to achieve? Are Jesus, Mohammed, the Buddha, Michelangelo, Leonardo Da Vinci, Mozart, and the Beatles just anomalies? Are we really created in God's image, and if so, are there some terrible design flaws? Or have we "created" God as an idealized image of ourselves — the way we really would like to be? Are we still paying the price for Adam and Eve's mistake? Or, more hopefully, are we on the verge of a new and better phase of evolution?

Do animals have a sense of conscience or compassion, and therefore some responsibility for the well-being of their neighbours? Consider the following poem:

Predators.

No predator
Killing its prey
Thinks of evil

Humanity created evil.
It first emerged
With knowledge of polarity.

Good and evil
Are polar opposites.
Above it all
Stands eternity.

God is *not* good.
Nor evil.
Creator of the predator
It Is.

To find answers to these questions we must go back
to our own pre-historic roots.

* * *

Part 2.
Claim Your Power.

7. Hunters - Gatherers.

The term hunter-gatherer is used to describe human beings who obtain their food from nature by hunting animals and gathering wild plants, fruits, etc.

Prior to an average 15,000 years ago, humanity lived this subsistence lifestyle of hunting, trapping, fishing and gathering. The task of the men was to hunt for meat (now replaced by money) and fight with neighbouring tribes (now government and corporation politics and aggression) for control of territory and food resources. The women would gather edible plants, fruits, mushrooms, etc., and bear and raise children.

These tribes were small, usually less than 30 people. They lived a nomadic existence and were constantly moving as local food resources were depleted. Agriculture had not yet been invented, and would evolve slowly through stages of pseudo-agriculture where nomads would burn areas of inedible plants to encourage edible ones. Even in agricultural societies people continued to hunt/fish and gather natural edibles.

Hunting-gathering tribes had few material possessions which all had to be carried with the constant moving around. The development of villages and eventually cities was not possible until the onset of agriculture evolved at the beginning of the Neolithic era, averaging 10,000 years ago. This development allowed for a greater and more reliable food supply. This also made the development of specialized skills possible; it is the period of history where skills such as blacksmithing and tool making first emerged.

Living the hunting-gathering life must have been extremely dangerous with only a club and spear and eventually a simple bow and arrow to defend oneself against animal predators and human raiders. Falling victim to lions, hyenas, bears, cougars, snakes, and packs of wolves must have been common. Fortunately for humanity, evolution provided some safeguards, the Flight or Flight Response, now generally referred to as the Fight, Flight or Freeze Response (the FFF response).

When faced with a potentially dangerous situation, we have three choices, fight the threat, flee from the threat, or freeze, i.e. remain motionless so that the threat may not be aware of us. These choices are made automatically and without conscious choice.

The physical processes of the FFF response are:

1. an external stress event is observed

2. the visual data are processed in the brain by the cortex, and

3. sent to the hippocampus to compare to memories of previous experiences

4. they are then sent to the hypothalamus which releases a substance (CRH - Corticotropin-releasing hormone) that triggers the pituitary gland.

5. the pituitary then releases a hormone (ACTH Adrenocorticotropicho-mone) which stimulates the adrenals.

6. these release corticosteroids (adrenalin and noradrenalin) which stimulate a number of physical responses (see below)

Adrenalin has the following physical effects:

Effects	Results
* Rapid breathing	>> Increases blood oxygen level
* Enhanced muscle tone	>> Ready for increased activity
* Blood circulation diverted	>> Shunts blood to major muscle groups
* Skin blood vessels constrict	>> Reduces blood loss from injury
* Stops digestion	>> Saves energy
* Stops liver, kidney function	>> Saves energy
* Suppresses immune system	>> Saves energy

* Dilates pupils	>> See clearly, better night vision
* Sweat glands open	>> Extra cooling of body
* Endorphins released	>> Minimizes pain effects

All these effects serve to get the body primed for high-energy physical activities: fight, run for your life or, if you have enough self-control, freeze. This was all very useful 15,000 years ago, but what about in the 21st century? Are we still stuck with an archaic safety device or have we outgrown it? The answer is: unfortunately yes, these safety devices are still present and active. We still have exactly the same archaic system operating in this supposedly modern world of ours . . .

Note: The processes described above are much simplified versions of very complex processes.

* * *

8. What is Healing?

Time is a curious concept. It is divided between the past and the future: events that have already occurred and those that have not yet happened. In between is a tiny pinprick of time that we call "the here and now". Whether this actually takes up a certain miniscule amount of time or is a timeless point in the continuum of time is debatable, but it is a fact that each person lives in "the here and now", and we have no choice in the matter. We can imagine past and future events and even experience the feelings and emotions that are attached to them, but in "real time" we are here and now.

This is a rational description of what we call linear time. It can be demonstrated in "real time", and surely a mathematician has already come up with a formula that demonstrates the reality of time. It is a rationalized "left brain" description of time. Of course there are no short and long hours; an hour is an hour and no amount of debate can make it longer or shorter. Once an event has occurred it is "history" and cannot be changed, What happens is irrevocable.

But this is not the way a person *experiences* time. We all know that some events of a defined length of linear time seems to last much longer or shorter than "real time". An hour spent with your true love seems to last only minutes; an hour spent in a war zone lasts for days. The way a person *experiences* time is an illusion; the experience of an event is a *perception* of what happens. The way different people experience a given event can be significantly different. An experience is useful to become fully aware of the factual and emotional contents of an event, and this may help a person achieve a more objective and balanced insight into the event. But it is not absolute and it is not unchangeable. What seems to last for hours at the moment of happening may later seem to have lasted only minutes.

A current or a past event can now be seen as consisting of two different aspects: the actual objective linear time occurrence, and the subjective experience of the event and its emotional impact. To the experiencer both aspects of the event are real.

The emotional/spiritual impact of an experienced-time event can be changed, which is especially important in the case of strong negative emotional memories that are the result of trauma. The "historical" linear-time event cannot be altered in any way *(although it's description can be changed of course, as has all too often been shown in history).

This can become a turning point in one's emotional/spiritual health. When the emotional content of a painful/stressful event has been "neutralized", the emotional charge of the memory will no longer negatively affect one's life: what one remembers becomes "just old neutral history".

This is one of the true definitions of "healing": to neutralize (or call it defuse) negative/stressful emotions for the purpose of improving one's physical, emotional, and spiritual health, thereby attaining a better quality of life.

This is not the same as curing which aims at reducing symptoms of, and eradicating disease, although healing can at times lead to the same result. Let us investigate in detail the possibilities of healing in the following chapter

*   *   *

9. Memories and Experiences.

According to the law of dependent arising, thoughts, emotions and actions do not exist under their own power. Everything is a result of something else, and matter, thoughts, emotions, and actions will result in yet something else again. How does this explain spontaneous (not previously considered) thoughts or actions that take place in the present moment?

What we see as spontaneous turns out to be motivated or caused by a previous event that we no longer have any awareness or memory of. Let me give a true personal example: many years ago I moved into a new apartment in a downtown high rise, a few blocks from the old city centre industrial airport. As the movers carried in my furniture, a plane just skimmed the top of the building on its final landing approach. Before I knew what I was doing I dove under the nearest table! The movers thought I was rather strange . . .

What was happening was a triggering of a decades old memory that propelled me under that table. That memory was from my adolescent years in my native Holland, occupied by the Nazis during the second world war, when regular air raids soon taught me to dive for safety. A memory of some 30 years ago and long forgotten. But was it really forgotten, or it was simply 'stored' in an subconscious part of my memory? Loud low flying plane = danger = dive for safety, activating a reflexive action to a different but similar situation, based on an old "forgotten" memory.

We can make a long list of uncomfortable, offensive, or traumatic experiences and their resulting motivations. These motivating energies may or may not be consciously known to the individual (or society), and sometimes they are simply avoided or ignored because they are too uncomfortable or painful.

Earlier on page 44 we noted: *"One observes, makes choices based on information collected, and makes decisions based on that information, insight, and understanding gained from previous experiences."* If these choices and decisions, whether remembered or not, are indeed based on previous events, they cannot be spontaneous. This raises some fundamental questions about memory and learned behaviour.

Memory is the ability of the brain (and other parts of the body) to save, store, and recall information about experienced/observed objects, events, thoughts, feelings, and emotions. Memory becomes more effective if the event has meaning. For example, an experience that happens in an environment that includes an aggressive animal will be more clearly and in greater detail remembered than the same environment without an animal; your friend's 10-digit telephone number is remembered much easier than a 10 digit series of random numbers.

If we were aware of all memories of an entire lifetime, our mental capacity and abilities would be seriously compromised by the unimaginable over-load of data. For that reason the vast majority of memories are stored in areas of the brain to which we have no immediate access. Only memories of experiences needed to conduct our daily life activi-ties are readily accessible;we do not have to take time out to re-think memories of repetitive daily tasks; we don't have to think about how to brush our teeth, such a routine habit is done "automatically"; we drive our cars mostly on "automatic pilot" and don't have to think about finding our way home . . . unless a traffic accident blocks our usual way and we have to think about finding a detour around the blocked street.

Accessing a memory that is "hidden" requires a stimulus to bring it back to consciousness, liter-ally a déjà vu - already seen, heard, smelled, felt, thought, sensed, experienced, etc.: "I'm sure I've seen him somewhere before", "when she said that it made me think of . . .. "

All that is safe and useful, but there can be prob-lems. Negative, painful, and traumatic experiences that have been "shoved under the carpet because they were too difficult, painful, or embarrassing to deal with, are not erased. They continue to persist in the unconscious mind and may result in chronic

stress which in turn depresses one's immune system and can cause serious health problems. The
longer we postpone dealing with painful memories,
the more difficult it will be to deal with their energies. At times it may take a powerful trauma (like a
terminal cancer diagnosis) to force one to come to
grips with those stored negative energies.

What happens when a stimulus, a current event,
re-opens a forgotten traumatic experience? We
tend to automatically respond in the same way we
did at the time of the original trauma, following
the scenario of the earlier experience. A somewhat comic example is me diving under a table
just because of the sound of a low-flying air plane.
The memories of air raids during the second world
war did not even enter my mind although they trig-
gered my instant action! That's fine as long as the
response is safe and not destructive (even if sometimes rather strange!).

If the reflexive response is negative, angry,
aggressive, or destructive, we may be in trouble.
Another serious aspects is that these reactions
seem almost impossible to control. The response
or reaction is instantaneous and not premedi-
tated. It seems to go off like an undetected bomb
and we have little or no control over its effects.
We may sadly regret it a minute later, but then
the damage has already been done. We will return
to this topic later to discuss what can be done
about this.

* * *

When I next stopped by at Mr. C.'s place we had an interesting conversation. I told him that I had discovered how I inherited some "values" from my ancestors, how I gained habits from my parents' examples, from my education and religious training, and many more influence from my own life experiences. And how some experiences, particularly the negative ones, continue to affect my thoughts and actions even after I have long "forgotten" them.

Mr. C sat quietly for a moment and then said: "you seem to have gained a lot of insight and knowledge about yourself and about life in general. Those are indeed insights that explain a lot about daily human behaviour. But as I said earlier, insights are little more than the ability (or is it a gift?) that "lets you peek behind a curtain"; they are not a solution to a problem."

"These are the fundamental causes and effects that create a dysfunctional personal life and, by extension, a dysfunctional society. Do we need to know all these reasons? Should we all undergo psychotherapy to unearth their origins? Should we feel sad or guilty about them? Should we just ignore them? Are we all going to be punished for that by ourselves, or by God, or through a reincarnation into an difficult or painful life?"

"Of course there is benefit in understanding what it is that makes us say and do the things we really don't want to say or do. Without that knowledge we would forever be driven by unknown forces. Going back in time and trying to *analyze* what happened is a "left brain" rationalizing experience that is often of little help, and may increase rather than release the emotional charge and guilt feelings. *Sharing* one's story, expressing feelings with words, and sharing them with a trusted person (not your immediate family members!) can be a powerful experience that may trigger a deep sense of release from the emotional charge. But it is difficult to let yourself be that vulnerable to another person, wondering what she or he is really going to think about you! We will address positive ways of dealing with trauma in Chapter 13.

* * *

10. About Energies.

There is still one question left about awareness and choice. We have talked about living entities: plants, and animals. We can safely leave inanimate objects - rocks, water, air, etc. - out of this equation. (I have never seen a rock make a choice although I sometimes wonder if, when I stub my toe on a rock, it had put itself in my path deliberately. . . But that is another story.)

Plants and animals all have one specific quality in common: they are all alive. If we all exist in dependence on our components, then is there really a fundamental difference between these categories? Some will argue that trees and plants, like all animals, indeed have some level of awareness, and this viewpoint is gaining popularity these days. But as far as we know, plants do not have the ability to collect and store information, and therefore cannot make conscious choices that produce change. Let's now take a closer look specifically at what it is that plants and animals have in common.

I have served for many years as a hospice volunteer, at times sitting overnight vigils with a dying person, and I have several times been present at the moment of death. Something curious and very tangible happens at that moment. It is very obvious that "something" leaves the body, something very noticeable and almost substantial. The body suddenly changes from an animated object into an empty shell, its "life energy" suddenly disappears, leaving the body behind as a mere object.

Is there such a "thing" as life energy? Can it leave and therefore must, at some moment in the past, have entered a body? It is remarkable that science still has not been able to define life. We know what life is - we all experience it daily. We know how it works and what makes it come and go: birth and death, but we don't know what it consists of. Looking at what animates life as "energy" may perhaps make things a bit easier to comprehend.

Here is a general description: *"Life is a characteristic that distinguishes objects that have self-sustaining biological processes from those that do not, either because such functions have ceased (death), or else because they lack such functions and are classified as inanimate."* [5] But it tells us nothing about what life really is and what it consists of. Do various energy forms, including life, arise dependently or independently; do these energy forms exist in their own right rather than depend on their components to exist? (exist, not manifest, which is a very different process). If those components change, would they thereby change the nature of the life energy, and thereby the manifestations of life itself ?

In physics, "fundamental interactions" [6] are the ways in which the fundamental particles of the universe interact with each other. An "interaction" is fundamental when it cannot be described as dependent on other interactions: when they are not dependently arising. The four known independently arising fundamental interactions are:

- gravity,
- electromagnetism,
- the strong nuclear force,
- the weak nuclear force.

These four energy forms are the most fundamental and timeless components of the entire universe, and all other energies and their manifestations derive from them.

It is interesting to note that the life force has not been included in that list of fundamental inter-actions. However, as we have not been able to identify even one component or process that is a component of the life energy we can only conclude that, for the time being at least, life must be an independently arising phenomenon. This would make life an eternal and unchanging force in the universe that will continue to exist unchanged for all time in the same manner as gravity, the electro-magnetic force, and the strong and weak nuclear forces. That means that life can be neither cre-ated nor destroyed, although its *manifestations* all end in destruction of course. Perhaps science will include it in the future when physicists have become interested in life as more than an observ-able phenomenon.

This reminds me of a poem I wrote several years ago, when I was puzzling over what life is all about:

The River.

The River flows eternally.
It never stops, reverses, or dries up,
And I am given time to dwell along its banks.

Created in its depth I crawled on shore.
All I could do was creep through muddy banks
Not knowing what would lie ahead.
And all was well as long as I crept on;
I was the crawling bug along the road of life.

Until one day I reached firm ground.
I turned around and could look back from whence
I came.
Fear clenched my throat, I'd gone too far!
Now, could I still return and join my source,
Or would true unity elude my search
While longing drives me on?

Now: I can think!
I want a guide so that I can retrieve
The path that leads to heav'n and bliss.

But God is giving me no answers.
All promised Good I cannot find,
And when I search the world around me
I only find the ugliness of ego-play.

And feeling lost, I vote security,
Please do not change that which I can still hold.
"I don't feel lost, I'm f-f-feeling fine, Sir. Thank
you".
And greed for goods and power drives me on

And all that time I roam along the bank and think:
If only I can learn to *understand*
I'll find the way to once again dive in
And swim.

But could I still get out?
Or drown? What would the neighbours think?
And merge into a timeless unity and lose control?!

How can I ever stop the need to understand
And just jump in and swim?

The River flows eternally.
It never stops, reverses, or dries up.
And I am given time to dwell along its banks.

Even if we don't know what life is, the universal life energy is shared by all life forms from one-cell organisms to elephants and trees. Taking this literally, this means that we are all remote "cousins", connected with each other by the phenomenon called life.

That is a wonderful insight that unfortunately is of little help when it comes to daily reality. We have no qualms about killing our cousin the mosquito, or the other cousin the flu virus. "Eat or be eaten" still takes precedence over looking after our "cousins".

Another interesting question arises when one wonders *why* science has not investigated what life really is. Life is after all an energy that we all experience daily. Left unanswered, it leaves a gap in our fundamental knowledge and understanding of ourselves and of the universe we live in and share with other forms of life. Coming to an understanding of what life is will most certainly have a fundamental impact on how we live our lives and how we relate to other living creatures.

A simple example may clarify this when we consider altruism. The usual definition of altruism is of course the performance of an action with no expectation of compensation or other reward in any form, whether it be money, gifts, admiration, fame and honour, or ego satisfaction. But let's leave the negative definition of "no expectation" behind, and instead focus on the fact that we all are manifestations of one indivisible life force.

True altruism is an expression of love, acceptance, and compassion, manifested as beneficial action of any kind. It appears when there is complete acceptance and unity between the altruistic person and the recipient.

Any reward of any kind is then completely meaningless, and the action is energized by the oneness of life itself. (We'll come back to this in chapter 20.) Would this perhaps be the true definition of what we call God?

The insight and awareness of this possibility can have the most profound impact on society if we can find ways to implement and practise it.

"We are being challenged to the next level of existence, the next stage in the evolution of ourselves and of the universe." [7]

* * *

11. About Dying, Death, and Grief.

How can we ever come to terms with a loss that is as irrevocable as death; how can we make sense of it; how can we deal with it? It's a question humanity has struggled with for thousands of years without really finding a clear answer to it, and will not find an answer till we learn to "make friends with death": to find ways to accept death without being overcome by overpowering emotions of loss. It is to learn to understand the phenomenon of life and its inevitable consequence: death.

Birth is understood as the start of a new life, and we happily celebrate it almost every time. But is that really true; is birth the start of a new life? Does life starts at the moment of conception, when a living sperm cell and a living egg unite? Those cells are indeed already living; if they were not, conception would not occur. This means that no *new* life is created. What is created is a new living cell that will multiply by cell division, and the newly divided cells will differentiate and develop into the multitude of different organs and functions. New life? No, "only" a new *manifestation* of life.

When a physical body begins to malfunction because of damage through accident or illness, or because of wearing out from ageing, it will eventually stop functioning: the ending of the manifestation of that life.

At death, when the life energy leaves the body, it leaves behind what is often called the physical remains. (such a literally correct term). We grieve the dead person's presence: their company, their love and friendship, their sharing, their wisdom and insights, and so much more. But have we lost their *energetic* presence or do we feel that loss because their *bodily* presence has ended? Does it mean that the deceased person has entirely left? Can we no longer communicate with them, can we no longer share our lives and our experiences, thoughts, and feelings with them? Have we really lost them?

* * *

If indeed life is an energy that leaves the body at the time of death, how does that affect the concepts of soul and spirit? Soul (derived from the Old English word "Sāwl" and the Latin "Spiritus") is variously defined as:

*   an non-physical essence,
*   an energizing cause,
*   an animating principle.

Spirit has a multitude of different definitions, including:

*   a spiritual principle embodied in humans
*   an essence, a principle, a cause
*   a specific inclination, disposition, or tendency
*   an energy that carries certain properties

These definitions within the context of life and death all point to a non-material quality: a form of energy imbued with a principle, an essence, an inclination, or even certain "specific "properties". This is perhaps analogous to electricity carrying messages as in modern electronic devices. Could it be that the life energy can carry "information"? Have we as human beings evolved far enough that this may be a possibility?

* * *

Now let's step beyond these theories and look at reality. If this were all true, then:

* is there anything that continues beyond physical death that carries certain properties and "messages" as defined above?

* does the life energy manifest more than once?

* what proof is there of that; why don't we remember previous lives?

1. Is there anything that continues beyond death?

If we accept the premise of life as a *fundamental interaction*, then this energy continues infinitely beyond death as it is independently originating, If it is unchangeable and timeless, it can in principle indeed carry certain properties and processes, including those of previous manifestations.

2. Does the life energy manifest more than once?

The life energy itself (not its manifestations) does not come in permanent discreet packages. It is universally and timelessly present, and at the time of all conceptions *manifests* in a multitude of different life forms whenever and wherever conditions are right.

3. Remembering our "past.

In general, the brain is the seat of many aspects of memory. They are the records of everything we do, say, think, feel, experience, and have learned. If the life energy can carry information beyond the end of a manifestation it follows that remembering past life events is not impossible.

There is a broad range of literature regarding memories from past lives, especially among small children, that includes both speculation, philosophy, and serious scientific investigation and tests. Your local library certainly will have titles which are worth reading, such as "They walk among us" [8] and "Many Lives, Many Masters" [9]

If the life energy at some previous time was present in another human body, that does not mean that it is the previous person who is now manifesting again; it is not "here comes Johnny again"! It is a new manifestation of life energy, not of the previous body.

Buddhists believe that after death a person enters a state of much chaos and confusion: the

Bardo state. Others believe that the essential person resides in another dimension. and projects itself into a physical expression. Both streams believe that the specific purpose is to ameliorate negative feelings, motivations, and acts. This process of reincarnation may have to be repeated numerous times until the desired state of positive energy (love, acceptance and compassion) has been achieved. Thus *reincarnation is a process of learning*.

It is worth noting that reincarnation was accepted by the early Christian church until the middle of the 6th century. Origen of Alexandria and several early saints such as as for example St. Augustin, wrote extensively on the subject in the third century.(Plato also wrote about it in detail in his *"Republic"*, written around 380 BC)

During a stormy and politically skewed second Council of Constantinople in 543 AD, the principle of reincarnation was rejected as being contrary to the resurrection of Jesus. Origen was declared a heretic and his writings were banned and destroyed. The Roman emperor Justinian at first rejected this, but later confirmed the rejection of reincarnation.

As to past life memories: advanced masters claim that they can access memories of past lives. Most people like you and I don't have that skill, probably for good reasons.

* * *

But if it isn't Johnny again, what specifically is it that continues after death; if reincarnation is real, why do most of us not remember previous lives?

There is one more aspect that is present in all human beings: the "essence" of a person. We have all met persons who gave the instant impression that they are angry, or kind, greedy, communicative, aggressive, compassionate, etc. It is not that this person always *acts* angry etc; it seems that anger is at the core of their very being. It is as if that trait is or has become his/her "second nature". It has become the "essence" of that person.

This individual essence, together with highly emotionally charged memories, becomes embedded in that person's life energy and, if they have not been resolved, will be carried forward into another life, whether again as an aggressive person (but not Johnny) or as an aggressive animal. (Always wanted to be a lion; here is your chance, but remember you may also show up as a mosquito!) The process of the same essence carried forward into a new body is called "karma". Karma is the law of cause and effect. It originates in a previous life, and may manifest during a future life time; the next life or a later one. Essentially it is the same cause and effect scenario as in "if you don't eat your spinach now you'll have to eat it tomorrow". When karma involves a special relationship such as between parents and children, or a controversy between two people, these people may in a future life meet again, thereby creating new opportunities to resolve their negative relationship.

Karma can be positive or negative, and it is not punishment for one's sins. It is more like a reflexive reaction to unresolved situations. For that reason the concept of judgment by a deity or other higher power becomes entirely mute.

Positive karma can be equally as strong as negative karma, so if you are a very compassionate person: hang on! Continue to practise compassion and you'll happily carry that forward into a next life as well.

But what to do about negative karma? The short answer is: "change it!" Easier said than done, but it can be done. Negative karma is the continuing expression of everything that is harmful to other living entities; fundamentally it is the expression of animal instincts as discussed in Chapter 7.

Negative karma is not fun, and it seems that many human beings have a wish to make things better and to correct those deficiencies. Karma gives one unlimited new opportunities to do that until the deficiency has been turned into a positive quality. And when finally, after many life times, all negatives have been transformed (for most of us that will probably take an awful lot of life times!), there is no longer a need to return again into a physical body unless one wants to come back again for the sole purpose of helping others achieve the same perfection: practising true compassion. The people who choose to return again to help others we call saints (such as Mother Theresa, Gandhi, the Dalai Lama, and many others). Buddhists call them Bodhisattvas

Examples of Karma:

Negative	Positive
control	freedom
sadness, regret	happiness
stress	relaxation
aggression	respect
polarity: "us and them"	compassion
fear and anger	freedom
judgment	acceptance
aggression	non-judgmental

Through the great gift of karma (although it can sometimes be pretty uncomfortable!) we have unlimited possibilities to become perfected. Karma is the mechanism that creates ideal learning opportunities.

The *meaning of life* is embedded in the human drive for a better world, to become completely altruistic; the *purpose of life* is to experience an unlimited number of karma-filled lives in order to evolve ever closer to that meaning of life.

In summary: the whole idea that we have only one physical life, fully loaded with basic animal drives and instincts, and that we have any hope of ending that life without having made major mistakes for which we are then judged, makes little if any sense. It must be a rare exception that any human being achieves such perfection in one lifetime. This whole concept sounds suspiciously like a scare tactic, designed to try and control human behaviour - a tactic that has obviously failed.

I am sure that upon death we review and evaluate - not judge - our own lives, become fully aware of our mistakes and shortcomings, and come back to try and correct those. Given the inborn load of instincts and drives, that may take many tries until we indeed arrive at a state where we no longer need to come back to bodily life. We have then learned the lessons for which we have come here to learn.

The responsibility is entirely ours!

* * *

12. Where Attention Goes, Energy Flows.

Where attention goes . . ? Let me give you a delicious example from many years ago. I still remember a science class in high school, where I just couldn't keep my eyes of a beautiful girl a couple of rows over. And it seemed that she surreptitiously kept watching me as well. I was about to wink at her when I heard the teacher say "Robert, pay attention!" I didn't know I was that obvious!

At the first opportunity I of course winked at her anyway, and she winked back at me. Which led to a date, which led to us going to a dance, which led to our first kiss (which I still vividly remember), which led to . . . oh, never mind! Where my attention went, energy was flowing pretty strong and obvious, and I got quite a ribbing from my friends during recess!

What is "attention"? The brain can receive many stimuli simultaneously through various sense organs. Focused attention is the ability to screen out all but a few selected stimuli. This is not necessarily at the expense of the other stimuli, but research has shown that the conscious part of the brain is most often not able to recall, process, and distinguish in detail too many simultaneous stimuli. Of course one can also focus on no stimulus or even no brain activity at all, as in deep meditation. But that requires a lot of practice because our brain is wired to be constantly on the look-out, and shutting down that busyness in favour of no stimulation is a tricky exercise!

Stimulated actions can be voluntary or involuntary, which can make quite a difference. In my example from my high school days, my staring and winking at that girl was pretty well involuntary, mostly driven by hormones I suppose. In case you doubt that, "I didn't know I was that obvious!" pretty well demonstrates that.

Seeing a threatening person near me immediately energizes my FFF response. It takes conscious thought to override that reaction and move my focus to a more rational response, for example "he's all talk and no action anyway".

I have attended many workshops, seminars, and retreats over the years, but what happens on Monday morning when my left-brain rationality takes control again? What happens then to that experiential knowledge that I gained during the weekend? How do I achieve a balance between rational *knowing* and experiential *knowledge* - how do I apply all I gained during that weekend workshop to everyday life?

Many self-help programs are based on making that choice of switching from involuntary habit to intentional action. Feeling depressed? Try and switch to positive thinking and you'll soon begin to feel better. Seeing yourself as a failure after your marriage has collapsed? Talk with a trusted friend about it to release some of the emotional pressure (putting words to feelings is magic), and then go to the gym for a good work-out. I'm sure we can all think of a hundred examples.

But what about things you can do nothing about? " I've just been diagnosed with cancer and the doctor gave me only one month"? At first glance not much you can do about that; surgery, chemo, radiation, and if that doesn't kill the cancer the rest can be pretty hopeless. Never mind staring at a pretty girl in high school, I am now staring at death.

Us human beings seem to have a tendency to focus on what we don't have: on negative things. (If you don't agree, just watch the evening news). Read the Coffee Maker story again. Here is Mr. Wishing again, in a negative mood this time:

- continue wandering around in a forest but I can't find my way out anyway.

- let's build a cabin; but of course I forgot to bring my darn tools.

- hey, there's a rabbit; how useless is that?

- here is the end of the forest; hundreds of opportunities and choices, nice coffee shop. Here is an opportunity to start my own business, but of course the guy won't give me his coffee maker.

- more wandering. Hey, there is an empty little shop with all the materials for making a coffee maker. But darn it, no tools again!

Finally, Wishing gave up and changed his focus away from thinking and wanting things. He gave up trying to control his circumstances and got in touch with his feelings instead, "he felt defeated and cried".

When one stops wandering around in dark forests and wanting things; when one changes one's focus from self-centred thoughts to focusing on the reality that one cannot control life's circumstances, that is when things begin to change. A true change of focus from control to freedom changes the quality of the energy flow from negative to positive.

How does that apply to having cancer? Remember how in the days and weeks after my surgery I let my mind run through a whole gamut of questions and thoughts until I finally gave up when I realized that there are no rational answers to irrational happenings? To this day I still don't know what actually happened, and it doesn't really matter anymore. I switched my attention from all those rational questions about what happened and why, to the open-ended question of what I want to do with my days for the rest of my life, no matter how long or short that may turn out to be. And that shift of focus took a very big bite out of my fear of death and dying.

How does that apply if you who have been diagnosed with a potentially fatal disease? Do you want to focus your attention on the disease and on all the negative effects it has on your life and the lives of those around you, and on the "fact" that you may die within the next few months? Or do you want to make the changes you are looking for? A cure may or may not be in the cards for you, but if you are willing to make the changes that you *can* make, you are on the road to healing. (See Chapter 8 again).

Consider supporting others around you, be available to those who are struggling with cancer, and help them with their fears and pain. Organizations such as the local chapter of the Cancer Society, your local hospital, the Red Cross, or a Hospice Society are good places to start. Choose that route and, almost magically, the fact that you may be dying soon isn't quite as overpowering anymore. . .

* * *

You may well ask, what did *I* do (rather than just talk about it) when I couldn't find answers to all my questions? Here are a few examples, and remember that this has been an ongoing process that is continuing to this day and into the future.

1. On the advice of a friend I started to swim several times a week to get myself back into good physical shape and dispel some of my anxiety energy.

2. I started restorative Yoga and doing muscle stretches, especially for my legs and back which were getting pretty tight after lying in bed for a long time.

3. I changed my diet, eating very little red meat, cutting way down on white sugar and other refined food stuffs. I also eat as much certified organic fruit and vegetables as I can find.

4. I learned to meditate. I now meditate for an hour every morning and evening. Yes I know, that is pretty time consuming, but it really helps me to keep my mind and thoughts "clean".

5. I started to volunteer at the Cancer Society, facilitating support groups for people who have cancer and others with severe chronic illness. I have presented a psychosocial oncology program for people with cancer and others with severe chronic illnesses at medical clinics and hospitals. Psychosocial Oncology is an aspect of cancer care that addresses the physical, psychological, emotional, social, and spiritual impacts that a persons with cancer and their family and care givers often struggle with. I eventually researched and wrote a program, called "Working with Cancer"© (see chapter 14) which I have presented to groups of people with cancer for some 15 years. This is also offered on an individual basis.

6. Watch your language! Focused thinking includes avoiding being against anything. Try not to be *against* war, *against* poverty, *against* cancer, *against* domestic violence. Instead think in terms of being *for* peace, *for* safety and security for everyone, *for* good health.

Avoid slogans such as "the fight against cancer" (the unfortunate slogan of the Canadian Cancer Society)."Fighting and "being against" are negative terms. Rather, support cancer research, and offer support and care to people with cancer and their families. In part as a results of this deliberate switch to focused thinking and action I have been free of cancer for more than 30 years, and I am in good health at age 82. Your choice of positive language, words, and topics has an enormous impact on your state of mind and your health!

I am not claiming that these forms of self-care are a cure for cancer. They are not. But I *am* claiming that this approach to healing, self-care, and compassionate service to others, has improved the quality of my life tremendously, which in turn has a beneficial effect on my health and my emotional and spiritual well-being.

"Where attention goes, energy flows". Positive or negative energy - your choice - flows to wherever you care to direct it. It's not easy to practise, and in the beginning it takes a lot of hard work and careful attention. But with effort you too can improve the quality of your life and the quality of the lives of your loved ones, thereby improving your physical, emotional, psychological, and spiritual health.

During a workshop many years ago I learned yet another simple truth, "if you don't *do* it, it doesn't count!" This simple sentence translates into: "you can talk about it all you want, but if you don't start actually *doing* it you are wasting your time!"

Stop endlessly wandering around in that dark forest of depression, hopelessness, and fear, and decide to switch your focus of attention to where you want it to be. You may not live forever, in fact your life may be shorter than you would wish it to be, but you can have a good quality of life while it lasts. And die in peace . . .

* * *

13. Chronic Stress.

It is no secret that our present lifestyle creates a lot of stress with all the resulting issues that derive from that. We are often so used to the frantic pace of life that we are not very aware of it, and one can daily observe how many people are obsessively looking for "more": more excitement, more activities, more entertainment, more sex, more everything, while finding little satisfaction and happiness in what they already have. They are adding to an already overburdened life in the false hope that they somehow will find the satisfaction and happiness they crave - if they could just run a little faster.

Chronic stress is not caused by a specific event, unless that event has not been effectively dealt with. It is usually the result of a continuously stressful lifestyle. There is a very graphic folk legend that demonstrates this difference: one frog is placed in boiling water, and another frog is placed in water that slowly comes to a boil. The frog in the boiling water immediately jumps out; the frog placed in the water that slowly comes to a boil lingers, never jumps out, and dies. This is how chronic stress is: gradually accumulating stress adds up without one being consciously aware of it; stress caused by a traumatic event catches our immediate attention and prompts us to deal with it.

All people have cancer cells in their bodies during the entire course of their lives. This is normal, and a healthy body takes care of these aberrant cells. An impaired immune system is one of the causes of the initial appearance of cancer, and its early slow growth escapes our attention until symptoms start to appear.

Stress is caused by the ways in which we perceive threats to our existence: our safety, our security, our well-being, and our happiness. Other negative experiences, as minor as they may seem to an outsider, can equally make a mess of our emotional life. For example, self-criticism; the disruption of normal family life with its severe impact on spouses, children, and parents; long-term changes in life style (job loss, physical disability); and deep-seated feelings of guilt or grief can trigger severe chronic stress.

As we already noted in chapter 9, emotionally painful traumatic experiences that have been pushed under the rug because they are too difficult or painful to deal with do not simply disappear. If not appropriately dealt with they eventually can cause suppression of the immune system which may result in chronic illness. The longer we postpone dealing with these emotions, the more powerful their energies become. This is why trauma counsellors are often brought in after disasters to help victims "defuse" the emotional charge of a traumatic experience. It is imperative for our health and well-being that we become more aware of our hidden fears and traumas, learn effective ways to defuse these emotions, and thereby avoid developing chronic stress and an impaired immune system with all the dangers that come with that.

Cancer and other stressors may be caused by a variety of factors. These include:

1. disturbed naturally programmed cell death and replacement,
2. genetic damage or mutation (can be inherited from parents)
3. certain viruses, such as the Epstein-Barr and the Human Papilom viruses,
4. the environment: pollutants, pesticides, natural toxins (arsenic, asbestos)
5. radiation: ultra-violet, gamma, electromagnetic fields, X-rays
6. hepatitis B and C (can cause liver cancer)
7. lifestyle: diet, smoking, drug abuse, sun exposure
8. emotional: chronic stress, guilt, resentment, self-talk, trauma
9. religion/spiritual doubts, lack of connectedness, lack of meaning in life.

Some types of cancer are caused by one specific factor: prolonged exposure to asbestos almost invariably leads to lung cancer; the human papilloma virus causes cancer of the cervix; prolonged exposure to direct sunlight can cause skin cancers. However, most cancers are caused by a combination of factors. But all cancers have one thing in common: they severely disrupt one's life, cause deep physical, emotional, and spiritual suffering, and the deep-seated stress that often continues throughout the course of the disease and beyond.

There are several steps one can take to deal with stressful situations:

1. cultivate objective awareness of your situation,
2. monitor self-talk,
3. become your own "observer",
4. share and talk with a trusted person; join a support group
5. seek help and support from a healthcare professional

In principle, these are relatively simple tasks; in practice they are sometimes difficult to pursue because of the never-ending demands and distractions of daily life, and of avoidance caused by the fear of having to face reality . . . Let's take a look at all this in some detail.

Awareness,

Awareness can be focused on an external event or object that can be perceived by the senses, or on internal states of thoughts, feelings, and emotions. These can be conscious or unconscious. A change in awareness changes the ability to consciously detect an external or internal event, and may change the judgment of its qualities and values. The Vietnamese-born Buddhist monk Thich Nhat Hanh is the author of a number of excellent books on the subject, and offers retreats at his monastery called Plum Village [10] in France, and around the world.

An easy way to start cultivating your awareness is by increasing your awareness of an object. For example, lighting a candle on your dinner table as a reminder of being aware of your meal, its nutritional qualities and taste, all the people who have laboured to provide all its ingredients and prepared your meal; chewing your food carefully and savouring its flavours; and being aware of how it allows your body to continue functioning; all this is an excellent and simple exercise in building awareness. Using a candle or any other object as a focal point is an effective reminder to stay focused and not let your mind wander from one topic to another and another . . .

Another less easy example is a conversation with another person. Even if you are quite interested in the topic of the conversation, your mind can easily wander off to "did I turn off the stove when I left home this morning?", "did I let the dog out today?", "is that meeting this afternoon or tomorrow?", "I should not forget to pick up some groceries on the way home tonight" etc. etc. How can one's mind be so scattered . . ! Awareness building starts as an deliberate exercise; keep focusing on it, and you'll find that it will become a habit.

Much more difficult yet is to refrain from making assumptions. I have lost count of the number of times that I stopped listening to what someone else was talking about because I thought that I already knew what he or she was going to say next. I must be either very psychic (which I am not) or extremely rude and ignorant in my assumption that I already knew what was going to be said next!

The same for judgment, thinking or even interrupting a speaker with "I don't agree with what you are saying" before the speaker has even finished shows how arrogant and closed my mind can be! Or worse, say nothing and think, "boy, that person doesn't really know what she/he is talking about."

Self-talk:

Self-talk is literally talking to yourself, sometimes even out loud or at least mumbling, but mostly inside your own head, silently and persistently. Sometimes it seems that it never quits until you go to sleep or get involved in something very exciting that diverts your attention for a while. Alcohol and other drugs do that too. The worst of is that a lot of self-talk is negative stuff: self-criticism, critical thoughts about others even when you don't know the person (such as politicians), or even about situations that don't necessarily involve any persons at all.

It doesn't even have any entertainment value, so what is it good for? Well, it keeps you awake during the day and even in the middle of the night. It's a good avoidance that diverts you from more painful or upsetting thoughts and feelings; it allows you to say nasty things about other people in your mind so you never need to say it directly to the other person (unless anger takes over!); it makes you feel more powerful to "say" nasty things silently without having to face the consequences; and it gives you a relieving outlet for your bad moods. Are we having any fun yet . . ?

Oh, I forgot one more thing, it helps you filling up that empty void inside yourself, the void created by every-day routine blahs, by not seeing the beauty and value of life and nature (remember Mr. C's question about that in chapter 1 ?), by missing real community and friendships, even from feeling the lack of real romance (rather than watching romantic movies) that you felt during your courtship and honeymoon and that is now replaced with doing the laundry, cleaning the house, and endless supper preparations. Feel free to add your own favourite negatives to this almost totally endless list . . .

I hope that this is discouraging enough to interest you in looking for alternatives. Stop the self-talk! Simple, eh? A simple answer is to tell that little inner voice to **shut up!** every time you hear it. And surprisingly, it does that when you tell it that constantly. Not immediately: it is like a little child, you have to tell it several times before it really hears you, but eventually it will stop. I promise!

One little problem, "you must tell it to shut up *every time* you hear it . . . " That takes a lot of attention and awareness. We are so used to that little voice that we often pay little conscious attention to it, and often we don't even really hear it. And so it just goes on and on unchallenged. Guess what, here is where awareness practice pays off! Learn to be constantly aware. Start at meal time (remember that candle?), then at so many other daily routines, then . . . One can actually learn fairly quickly to "hear" it and, once that listening becomes a habit, to constantly tell it to stop - and it eventually will talk less and less and, during a good meditation, stops altogether. If you are a good stick-with-it person that should not be impossible; if you are not (yet) such a persistent person, prac- tise some more self-discipline, and pay attention!! (Ouch, sorry about that).

Become your own observer:

This in turn leads very nicely to the third point in the list: become your own observer. This will hap- pen almost automatically. As you learn to pay closer attention to when that inner voice pipes up again, it will begin to feel like you are almost "looking" at yourself. That habit can be broadened without too much difficulty. You will begin to notice when nega- tive thoughts or emotions enter your mind, and what your facial expressions and body language convey to others. Take a bit of distance; don't argue or fight; let those thoughts die a natural death. The most power- ful example of this that I have ever seen is of a friend of mine who quit smoking after more than 25 years of puffing, by saying out loud "stop it, STOP IT!!!" when reaching for the next cigaret. He hasn't smoked now for many years. (Or clap your hands, snap your fin- gers, or anything else that will really focus you). Yes, that's pretty dramatic, but it shows that it can be done: make up your mind what you want to do (we'll talk more about that in Chapter 20), keep a close eye on your mind and on that little inner voice, and refuse to go back to where you have really decided you don't want to be.

Remember, *where attention goes, energy flows!*

* * *

Another aspect of self-talk is going back over and over again to mistakes made earlier. It is easy to continue to fall into the trap of castigating yourself over bad thing you said or did, even when that happened decades ago. Once that becomes a habit it can be a real curse on everyday life. Asking the other person to forgive you or forgiving the other person is one potential solution, but even if that has been done and one has been forgiven, or you no longer have access to that person, the memory of the mistake or injustice can still linger on for a long time. Self-talk can be very persistent.

Fortunately there is a solution that can be very successful. As an example, let's assume that you said something very unkind to another person 20 years ago. You have asked that person to forgive you and you are now again good friends, but the self-talk remains. What you can do is this: the next time that unkind conversation shows up again in your self-talk, rather than feeling badly about it and beating yourself up for your unkindness, shift your focus of attention to *how you would have liked to have spoken* to your friend at the time of that event. Then (in your mind of course) replay that conversation the way you would have liked it to be. As you rehearse that new improved conversation, *focus on the feelings* that the conversation generates. If the "old" conversation was unkind, the new one will surely be much kinder; if you found yourself too judgmental in the old conversation you surely will feel more compassionate in the new one. Notice that and say to yourself, "I am now a kind/compassionate person". You may have to do this several times before that new and kinder conversation takes root and starts to replace that old unkind one, but with persistence it will happen.

Another way of dealing with negative self-talk is to forgive yourself for your mistake, your nasty comment, or whatever it was. There are many ways of doing this. You may find the following prayers/mantras helpful:

- May I be forgiven for all my imperfections and all my wrong-doings in thought, speech and action.

- Whatever I have done to hurt or offend another being, whether intentionally or unintentionally, may I be forgiven for that.

- I freely forgive all those who knowingly or unknowingly have caused pain, isolation or separation in me.

- May all beings be forgiven for all their imperfections and all their wrong-doings of thought, word, or action.

- Whatever any being has done to hurt or offend another, willingly or unwillingly, knowingly or unknowingly, may they be forgiven for that.[11]

When you continue to respond to negative memories in this way every time an old negative event pops up in your mind, replace it with the much more acceptable statement. In other words, change the language and/or actions of the event into the way you would have liked them to be in the first place, and your criticizing self-talk will change into a kinder scenario too. You will soon find that the old negative memory begins to fade and that you will indeed become the much better, kinder, considerate person you want to be.

Awareness, self-talk, observer. It's as simple and as difficult as that. Read Appendix A about meditation again. Meditation will probably start to make a lot more sense as a way to gain control over this threesome.

* * *

Part 3.
Gain your Freedom

14. Working with Cancer ©

"Everything that You Already Have"

"**Working with Cancer©**" is a program for people with cancer and their family members and other care givers. Based on research conducted at the Ontario Cancer Institute/The Princess Margaret Hospital in Toronto by a team of scientists headed by Alastair Cunningham, O.C., PhD. C.Psych, it was further developed in 1998 by Robert Rensing and presented over the years to hundreds of people with cancer.

The objectives of the program are to present clear and objective information in understandable language to persons with cancer about:

- the nature of cancer
- the physical, emotional, psychological, and spiritual impact of the diagnosis
- the progression of the disease that may be expected
- return to a normal lifestyle after remission or cure;
- death and dying.

The purpose of this information is that people with cancer and their loved ones have a clear and factual understanding of the disease and of what to expect, and to gain practical skills to deal with the enormous impact a cancer diagnosis can have on one's life.

Topics of the program include understanding of and insights into:

- what cancer is and is not,
- the factors that contribute to the onset and progression of cancer,
- an understanding of the impact of cancer on quality of daily life, how to deal with all that information and changes, and with the many aspects of spirituality from religion to atheism,
- practical tips about how to to talk with your family, your children, and doctors, and how to ask questions and remember the answers.

Presentations and exercise topics include relaxation, meditation, visualization, exploring lifestyle changes, goal setting, how to deal with the emotional impact of a cancer diagnosis, how to live constructively with a potentially life threatening disease, and honest and unbiased discussion of issues of religion, spirituality, and death and dying.

The entire foundation on which the *Working with Cancer*© program is based, is summed up in the following 500 year old poem. We ask that you spend some quiet time with this poem and fully absorb its meaning.

There is nothing I can give you
Which you do not already have;
But there is much, very much that,
While I cannot give it, you can take.

No heaven can come to us
Unless our hearts find rest in today.
Take heaven !
No peace lies in the future
Which is not hidden in this present instant.
Take Peace !

The gloom of the world is but a shadow.
Behind it, yet within reach, is joy.
There is a radiance and glory in the darkness,
Could we but see,
And to see we have only to look.
I beseech you to look.

Fra. Giovanni, A.D. 1513

The entire poem is summarized in the first two lines, "*There is nothing . . . which you do not already have*". In other words, you already have the innate potential for everything that you need for healing. If you find this poem powerful, what then is stopping you from gaining your freedom - from fear, from suffering, from worries, and from so many other negative and painful things?

In Chapter 8 we have already looked at the concept of healing. Healing of course is not the same as curing. Curing is the elimination of a disease or disability. Western medicine often uses a substance (medications) or intervention (surgery and therapy) to achieve cure. Unfortunately there are only limited cures yet for various chronic illnesses such as cancer, multiple sclerosis, muscular dystrophy, and Crohn's disease. This is where healing offers valuable supplements and alternatives. Please remember that healing is *never* a poor second choice for curing.

The power of healing is enormous, regardless of whether or not cure is available or possible. It entails the entire body, mind, and spirit complex, rather than "merely" the repair of a malfunctioning part of the physical body. Just as non-physical afflictions such as chronic stress can have an enormous impact on the start and the progression of disease, the elimination of such afflictions can contribute powerfully toward curing of the disease and, whether or not cure is possible, toward a good quality of life and a peaceful dying process and death.

What that *"everything that you already have"* consists of is a difficult question to answer because the English language doesn't really have a word to describe it. Just as we use the term "mindset" for a state of mind that facilitates or influences the way we think and perceive, let's coin the word "Spirit Set".

Spirit Set can be defined as the perception of and insight into the meaning, purpose, and functioning of life. It includes the difference between an ego-centric and a compassionate view of life; between a materialistic and a spiritual understanding of the universe we live in; between an environment of isolated individualism, and community; between consumerism, and simplicity. In other words, it reflects an understanding of life in the many ways that are expressed in daily living.

All the "ingredients" that make up a positive Spirit Set are fundamentally part of humanity; they are the " . . . *nothing that you do not already have*" - the *"everything that you already do have"*. That allows each one of us to make choices and decisions about what the make-up of our spirit-set will consist of, and serious chronic illness may prompt us to start looking at those choices and eventually decide what is most relevant to each of us individually.

Consumerism has instilled in us a false sense of entitlement: I want a bigger house, I want a bigger car, I want a bigger TV, etc. It is not the bigger house or TV that is the problem, it is the "I want" part that is causing so many problems. It is the egocentric false sense of entitlement - the "I want" that damages our sense of community and our happiness. Everyone is entitled to food, shelter, and safety; no-one is *entitled* to a bigger house or TV; that has to be earned. The problem lies in the emphasis on "I" that seems to be replacing "we" in our western culture.

When cancer or another chronic disease strikes, "I" all of a sudden feels threatened and becomes fearful: "what is going to happen, how painful is this going to be, what is death and dying like, is there a judgment day coming up, what have I done wrong in my life to deserve this fate?" Those are the kind of questions that all-of-a-sudden become foremost in a person's mind. The mind and the spirit have all become affected by the disease. Consequently, as mind and spirit begin to heal again as a result of a changing spirit-set, the body will also reflect that healing. The body may perhaps have become too damaged for a full cure, but one's quality of life, peace of mind, and commitment to a physically, socially, mentally, and spiritually healthier lifestyle will have a profound effect on the quality of the remainder of one's life.

In the case of cancer, making the choice of learning new coping skills or modifying current ones, and its expression in the practice of spirituality, community, and compassion can make an enormous difference in whatever time a person may have left in his/her life.

To paraphrase the poem: the practical application in one's life of *"There is much . . . that you already have . . ."* may be found in the 2nd last line: *"And to see [it] we have only to look"*.

That is Healing - if you make that choice.

The entire purpose of the *Working with Cancer©* program is to facilitate healing, trusting that the powers of healing will make a substantial contribution to curing, and to increasing quality of life - to the total of our potential physical, mental, emotional, and spiritual health, waiting to be realized.

* * *

15. Existential Distortion.

"To be ignorant of what happened before you were born is to remain always a child."
Cicero

In Chapter 13 we talked about chronic stress, but there is still a more insidious source of stress that is always unknown to the person experiencing it. It originates at the very beginning of life, so let's start at the "beginning".

Animals have it easy. At mating time the male goes through his instincts-driven motions while mostly the female stands passively. Emotions do not appear to play a part in this ritual. After giving birth most mothers display an instinctual protective behaviour, and more highly evolved animals teach their young the necessary survival skills. After the young leave the nest and mature, often very quickly, no emotional bond appears to remain. Among some animals the bond between the male and female continues but it does not appear to be of an emotional nature.

This strategy does not apply to humans. The process of fertilization, conception, birth, and raising the young is entirely different. The whole process is imbued with emotion. One of the most significant and least understood and studied components is the emotions that surround and influence conception.

Although the sexual act by itself is by-and-large instinctual, the emotions prior to and during inter-course are very powerful indeed and, at the time of conception, have a powerful impact on determin-ing the "existential quality" of the fetus and the individual's childhood and adult life. "Existential quality" refers to the absorption by the unborn child of the emotions and actions that take place in its externally surrounding environment,

Emotions surrounding the sexual act, concep-tion, and gestation can range from anger, fear, revulsion, rejection, and hatred, to joy, love, hap-piness, compassion, and gratitude. Even during the instinctual part of the sexual act these emotions can be very strong and all-pervasive, and carry an enormously powerful impact on the fetus during and following conception. At the moment of con-ception more happens than merely physical concep-tion when sperm and egg merge. The positive or the negative emotional state of the mother and of those in her environment is absorbed by the embryo as well. If the emotional environment is very negative, the life energy of the embryo can become severely compromised.

Before proceeding we need to establish two facts. There can be no doubt that,

1. like all cells in our bodies, both sperm and ovum are alive and combine into one living entity at the time of conception.

2. memories of events that happened a long time ago are retained and can be recalled into consciousness. While an unborn infant is not able to recall his or her experiences during gestation, he or she lives during those moments and has psychological and/or physiological responses to them, which may influence the ongoing development of the brain structures and the mind of the child.

Research has shown that the effects of actions and emotions surrounding the fetus can influence all aspects of the health of the child (see Appendix D). For example, during pregnancy up to 25% of women experience anxiety and depression. When conception occurs in an atmosphere of rejection, the embryo cannot assign these feelings to a specific source; it cannot know that the feeling originates with for example the mother, since the fetus does not know that there are persons in its "external" world. It therefore *experiences* rejection and, if not eventually resolved, that may be something that will be carried for its entire life.

The same process occurs when the mother is happy with her pregnancy, when she treasures the child she is carrying, when she sings to it, when she tells stories to it, and shares with her child how happy she is. The child will then more likely be borne as a happy child, and is likely to become an adult who perceives the world as a happy and welcoming place. Of course there are other influences as well, such as inherited karma, as already discussed in chapter 11.

In contrast, a fetus that has experienced and formed its reality as one of rejection may become an adult that does not relate easily to others and is always sensitive to rejection. It may have a happy experience of closeness and acceptance when he meets the boy or girl of his dreams, marries her, and has a wonderful honeymoon. But when every-day reality sets in again, he may become more and more emotionally remote, and is less likely to become a loving caring parent.

He eventually may be tempted to look outside of his marriage for the closeness that he is missing, not realizing that it is he who has blocked feelings of closeness and acceptance because of his unconscious reality. No matter what he turns to for relief from his loneliness, the sense of rejection and being unworthy may follow him throughout his life, and his most fundamental world view may never change because he has no conscious awareness of those ancient hidden feelings.

I call such an unfortunate and painful life scenario "existential distortion".[12] It is fundamentally different from chronic stress which is caused by ongoing stressful experiences after birth and throughout life. One can become aware of chronic stress in a relatively easy way, for example by a friend or therapist pointing out that "when you do . . . it seems to create a lot of stress". Existential distortion is different in that the source and the ongoing presence of that stress-causing condition is virtually undetectable by the person affected by it. It is very difficult to become intimately aware of one's "life script", one's inner reality before birth, and it is therefore much more difficult to change and treat.

Can a person ever become aware of existential distortion; can it ever be changed; can a person ever become aware of this condition and thereby attempt to change it? At times psychotherapy or hypno-therapeutic regression may have an effect and may be able to modify the symptoms of this condition. Perhaps those therapies may even be able to open up that existential distortion, but that may take an awful lot of time and work.

Opening up the condition of existential distortion may happen during or after a severe trauma. Cancer, other serious chronic diseases, and other traumas such as a serious accident, the death of a parent, spouse, or a child; the loss of an important job, or the impending dissolution of a relationship, may sometimes be the trigger to that process of self-discovery.

A vivid real-life example is of a person during an impending divorce, whose reality-world consisted of one rejection after another (mostly self-imposed but the person wasn't aware of that). A mutually agreed-upon trial separation finally brought it to his attention that he either had to accept yet another feeling of rejection, or start looking inside himself and discover why his life seemed fraught with rejections. This person was fortunate in that through hypnotherapy the trial-separation actually led to that self-discovery. When this choice led to a process of self-discovery and realization of a distorted "inner reality", a series of very vivid dreams opened up his subconscious memory of a pre-natal childhood emotional environment of rejection. That was the person's unquestioned world; that was the way life was; that was his fundamental reality! Experiencing that insight in the most vivid manner during dreams finally gave him the power to "reject all rejections". It was an exquisitely painful experience in which both his own life and the life of his parents were exposed in all their raw emotions. But he stuck it out and in the end discovered that the imagined rejection that caused the failure of the marriage was sourced in his parents' rejection of him, and not in his imagined lack of being worthy and acceptable. His personal history was one of "inviting" others to reject him because of his own feelings of lack of self-worth and the resulting behaviours.

Upon returning home to his relationship, it blossomed into a very close and happy sharing of their lives. He will always have to be aware of his heritage of rejection feelings and behaviours, but with that, constant awareness of that his life and the lives of those around him have permanently changed into a happier and trusting life. He now has the tools to deal with those influences.

Exactly the same can happen to a person when she/he has been diagnosed with cancer. Although the triggers of various forms of cancer are many and may depend on multiple causes, one's "life script", including existential distortions, may be one of the conditions that influence the onset of cancer. Deep insight into those conditions may result in improved health. When dreams start to occur, pay very close attention to them; they can reveal or describe vital information. Awareness-building exercises and meditation can be of great help as well in discovering a more realistic insight into oneself and open up avenues toward dealing with the origins of cancer.

This is not to indicate that a major cause of cancer can be found in existential distortions, but existential distortions may turn out to be one of those factors, and can sometimes play a decisive role.

* * *

16. Many Paths, One Truth.

**" . . . life has a purpose
and everyone [is] born
to go on a kind of quest
to find that meaning."**[13]

The human environment of "dog eat dog" has
not changed much over the ages, and the instincts
and resulting attitudes and behaviours remain the
same: compete for energy, territory, dominance,
and mates. The only thing that has changed fundamentally is our increased awareness that dog-eat-
dog is not a happy environment in to live our lives
in. Somehow there must be a better way and a better world.

Unfortunately we have not yet found the tools
needed to achieve that happy world. We talk about
it frequently, from criticizing "the government" to
telling everyone else to make the changes we want
but often don't make ourselves. Another answer is
of course to do nothing, evade the whole issue, and
find our satisfaction and happiness in "things", life-
styles, toys, busyness, etc.

Yet another solution: if we cannot be happy and
satisfied in this life, there must be a happier one
just around the corner. And so we create "heaven",
surely a heavenly place to be where everyone is

permanently happy and satisfied with everything. . . Unless one misbehaved in one's current life, for which one must then pay the price of punishment. This has been, and still is, a very popular concept and a generally satisfactory(?) answer to our dog-eat-dog existence on earth.

Buddhism is a philosophy of life, discovered and proclaimed by a human being who is now called the Buddha. It places responsibility for one's behaviours and actions squarely and totally on the shoulders of each individual. Life is to be repeated again and again until the lessons of correct thought, emotions, and behaviour, have finally been learned (karma and rein-carnation). No promises about a nicer life after death.

"In Buddhist ethics, the code of conduct, set forth by the Buddha, is focused on the welfare and happiness of all beings everywhere. The disciplines and insights required for reaching that goal are like a raft by means of which one crosses a river. They are means to an end which . . . one takes [to] approach that [goal]." [14]

According to Buddhism, suffering is unavoidable on this earth (difficult to disagree with!). All other animals don't have that option of working towards happiness. As an example, those of you who have watched the famous BBC series *the Blue Planet* may remember a scene in which a snow leopard chases a gazelle in the Himalayas. When the gazelle is caught it lets out a heart-rending cry as it falls and becomes the leopard's lunch. Such is nature, unaware of the other, not kind, and not compassionate. Humanity is very fortunate to have access to a way out of that kind of suffering.

Many Paths, one Truth. Is this what ultimately distinguishes humanity from the animal world? It seems that every human being, whether aware of it or not, has an innate need and drive to make sense out of his or her environment and existence. In this context meaning is the opposite of random which is portrayed by "just living until time runs out". Meaning can include just about anything, from power, money, and fun; to community, love, and compassion, or becoming a hermit. (The latter does not exclude fun but hermits don't chase after it).

Purpose and meaning are different concepts. If purpose indicates a goal to be achieved, meaning indicates the contents and quality of the process of living. Religion and spirituality can provide a model that can be used to shape that process. Thus, spirituality, religion, and meaning are closely related. If one confuses meaning with purpose, and thereby equates religion and spirituality with purpose, a mental rigidity may set in that short-circuits life and its quest for meaning.

The expressions of the religious/spiritual world are complex. They include strictly codified religions that require unquestioned acceptance of a creed in order to belong, which in turn may give one exclusive access to heaven.The other extreme includes the re-thinking of spirituality that sometimes can lead to pretty interesting concepts from an external entity such as Nature and Mother Earth, to a supernatural object such as the moon, and to stating that the power and discipline of the mind are the very foundations of health and happiness.

"Many paths"; whether all those paths lead to the one Truth that points the way to meaning, purpose, and happiness in life is debatable. Undoubtedly there are numerous paths, wherever they may lead, even if some of those paths lead to dead ends rather than to truth.

"One truth" is more complex, unless we can all agree on what we mean by "Truth". Some may argue that Truth is the attainment of perfection; others may claim that complete submission to the powers of an external deity leads to ultimate Truth; yet others claim that Truth is attained by the unselfish practice of love and compassion. But all these indicate what to *do* in order to attain Truth.

But what *is* Truth? Does it consist of a variety of individual insights and understandings or is there a fundamental Universal Truth? Is it similar to knowing how Life expresses itself in myriad forms, but not knowing what that life energy ultimately is?

If we replace the word 'truth' with 'ideal' it becomes a bit more manageable. Perhaps "one Universal Truth'" does not exist any more than one universal set of morals and values, as it does not take the many and sometimes very different cultures and societies into account. Perhaps there is no real need for universal truth to exist as much as we may wish for that.

One ideal: the ideal of a better, kinder, peaceful, compassionate world; yes, that seems to be an almost universal ideal that most religions and spirituality streams aspire to. Whether or not it is achievable remains to be seen, and in the short term that is perhaps impossible until we have outgrown our dog-eat-dog attitudes! But if humanity really aspires to that ideal, perhaps there is still hope for the future. Do we perhaps all aspire to travel that path that leads to the Ultimate, in whichever way or form we understand that to be? Can a universal ideal replace universal disagreement?

* * *

Let us for a moment consider the model of the seven major chakras. A chakra is like a highway interchange where traffic from many directions converges. Chakras are points in our body where energies "converge"; they are the major "intersections" of the life energy. There are numerous such chakra points throughout our body, including seven major ones.

If one takes the numbers one to seven, the centre of that series is the number four,

<u>1 - 2 - 3</u> - **4** - <u>5 - 6 - 7</u>

The first three numbers 1, 2, and 3 represent the connections with the physical world:

1. the connection of the body to the physical world (the earth)

2. procreation, the continuation of physical life

3. the physical functioning of the body

Starting from the other end, the numbers 7, 6, and 5 represent the connections with the spiritual woprld:

7. the connection with the non-physical world,

6. communication with the non-physical world,

5. the connection between, and sharing with the physical world.

In the centre of it all stands 4, the heart chakra, where these two worlds "live" together, and where one can find hope, trust, and compassion.

CHAKRA	LOCATION	FUNCTION
1. root	- base of spine	-grounding to the earth, fear, sur- vival, FFF response
2. sacral	- pelvic bone	-sexuality, creativ- ity, desire, lower emotions
3. solar plexus	- three fingers width above the navel	- personal power, anger, gut feelings
4. heart	- centre of the chest	- higher emotions, love, compassion

5. throat	- below the lower jaw	- communication,
6. third eye	- two fingers above the nose bridge	- vision, dreams perception, wisdom, clairvoyance
7. crown	- centre of the top of the head	- universal insight, unity, spiritual wisdom.

Our culture tends to connect the heart with romantic notions, but the image of the heart: two lobes at the top ending in a point at the bottom, is merely a symbol. It doesn't even look like a physical heart which is a rather shapeless muscle with a lot of blood vessels around it, and that acts as a pump. But the notion of love that is attached to the heart harbours perhaps more intuitive wisdom than we are generally aware of. The heart stands at the centre of our two realities, the physical (external) and the spiritual (internal) worlds, and thereby stands at the very centre of human reality. It requires the awareness of *all* the other chakras for the heart chakra to be fully functional, including all positive and negative aspects of these realities. The balanced combination of the positives and negatives of body and spirit expresses itself in love and compassion.

Western culture wants us to believe that it is the mind that has initiated and produced so much progress: technology, material wealth, modern medicine, and an unprecedented high quality of life (to name but a few). These are only the physical

qualities of life that have increased so dramati-
cally. Relatively little attention is paid to spiritual
qualities. (In today's news I heard about a riot in
front of a store that started to sell the new iPhone;
people were fighting to get into the store first. I
have never seen a riot erupt to get into a church
or a meditation retreat first.) You may notice that
the mind is not even represented as a chakra and,
appropriately according to ancient wisdom, does
not warrant such a position. The mind by itself produces only false images and rationalizations, which
present only short-term satisfaction. How long
does the excitement of your new car lasts before
it becomes routine; how long does your brand-new
marriage euphoria lasts till every-day routines take
over? Only the heart produces the love, compassion,
and acceptance which are the sole building blocks
of lasting happiness. Happiness and short-term satisfaction are not the same thing!

What are love, compassion, and happiness, you
may ask? The simple and straightforward definitions
are:

1. love is the ability of being actively aware of
   the feelings, emotions, and needs of others
   (including oneself)

2. compassion is the ability to respond in a
   positive, supportive, non- judgmental, and
   unselfish manner to those feelings and needs.
   Again: including yourself!

3. Happiness is the practical result of the practise of love and compassion.

4. In order to remain, love and compassion must be free of judgment (of self and others).

This description of the understanding and functioning of the seven chakras, and the definitions of love, compassion, and happiness comprise the entire foundation of a fully and healthily functioning human person, which in turn results in a fully functional society and culture. It can be found in one form or another in religions and non-religious spirituality, although unfortunately it is not always practised.

* * *

17. Religion and Spirituality.

In view of what is written above regarding the chakras, love, and compassion, the concepts of religion and spirituality can take on a new meaning. The following excellent definition can be found in Wikipedia.[15]

"Spirituality can refer to an ultimate or an alleged immaterial reality, an inner path enabling a person to discover the essence of his/her being; or the deepest values and meanings by which people live, including meditation, prayer and contemplation. They are intended to develop an individual's inner life. Spiritual experience includes that of connectedness with a larger reality, yielding a more comprehensive self with other individuals or the human community, with nature or the cosmos, or with the divine realm. Spirituality is often experienced as a source of inspiration or orientation in life. It can encompass belief in immaterial realities or experiences of the immanent or transcendent nature of the world."

Here the focus is not on whether God does or does not exists. The focus is on the reality of: " . . . *an inner path enabling a person to discover the essence of his/her being; or "the deepest values and meanings by which people live . . . "* [16]

Compare this to definitions of religion in the following quotations:

"God is most often conceived of as the super-natural creator and overseer of the universe. Theologians have ascribed a variety of attributes to the many different concepts of God. The most common among these include omniscience (infinite knowledge), omnipotence (unlimited power), omni-presence (present everywhere), omnibenevolence (perfect goodness)," [17]

"God has also been conceived as being incor-poreal (immaterial), a personal being, the source of moral obligation and the "greatest conceiv-able existent". These attributes were all sup-ported to varying degrees by the early Jewish, Christian, and Muslim theologian philosophers, including Maimonides [18] and Al-Ghazali". Religion can be perceived as ". . . an orientation system that helps to interpret reality and define human beings." [19]

Greg M. Epstein, a humanist chaplain at Harvard University states that *"essentially all the world's major religions were founded on the principle that divine beings or forces can promise a level of justice in a supernatural realm that cannot be perceived in this natural one."*

If, according to this last quote, *"all the world's major religions"* believe that in this world: *"a level of* [true] *justice . . . cannot be perceived in this natural one"* indicates that there is no hope for a better world here on earth, perhaps those religions need to be re-examined. Let us not allow ourselves to fall into the trap of hopelessness because some religions say so.

And then there is non-religious Buddhism: *"The sole aim of spiritual practice is the complete alleviation of stress (called Nirvana) in Samsara (the physical world)."*[20] ?*The Buddha neither denies nor accepts a creator,"*[21] *"denies endorsing any views on creation,"*[22] and states that *"questions on the origin of the world are worthless. Dogmatic beliefs in a Supreme God are considered to pose a hindrance to the attainment of nirvana, the highest goal of Buddhist practice."* [23] "Theravada Buddhists view the Buddha as *"a human being who attained nirvana or Buddha hood, through human efforts"*.[24]

I propose that the Wikipedia definition of Spirituality by far overshadows the definitions of Religion as it applies to the wish to create a better world in the here and now. Mind games such as debating who created the world and whether God is omniscient are divisive and meaningless in the context of how we can create a better world.

* * *

Why did it take an experience of terminal cancer to come to this rebellious position? Living a materially comfortable and egocentric life is not conducive to paying attention to that "ultimate or alleged immaterial reality"; why pay attention to something one doesn't feel the need for in one's life? To make that transition to paying attention often requires a good "shake up".

When that shake-up finally occurs, sometimes one has to face a long list of unanswerable questions and a long period of discovery and learning. A good teacher or guide can be most useful, but it is not impossible to do it alone - with a lot of persistence and stubborn not-giving-up! And, without a teacher or guide, the end result can sometimes be quite unconventional and "interesting".

The world we live in today is not a very happy one. Is it not time that we start to ask the uncomfortable and unconventional questions about what it ultimately takes to create a better world?

* * *

Talking about spirituality is not all that far removed from talking about dying and death. Referring back to chapter 10 about life energies, death is "merely" the end of a physical manifestation of life energy.

During one's lifetime every person experiences an almost endless number of experiences, thoughts, and emotions. Whether these are remembered verbatim is a question that cannot be answered. We know that sometimes the *scenario* of a long forgotten experience emerges again, but mostly these memories seem to have disappeared. But the feelings, the "qualities" of experiences remain, and some at times can become cumulative. For example if we tend to respond to uncomfortable or challenging situations with anger, we may become an angry person; when we respond in a despondent manner and blame ourselves even if the blame lies elsewhere, we may become a depressed person. These ongoing cumulative qualities become the person's "personality traits". They become the way the person is in daily life, his/her inner reality as felt internally and noticed by others.

According to Buddhism, these "qualities" remain after death and may be carried forward into a next life. Others believe that memories from a previous life experience can be recalled in a future life through the abilities of a psychic medium or through the use of time regression hypnosis.

According to various religions a deceased person will at some time be judged for his or her mistakes and on the effects that these mistaken actions or thoughts had on other persons. The judgment may result in punishment and further suffering. One problem with this belief is that, if the memories and "qualities" of past wrongdoings are erased when the brain dies, then on judgment day that person would not be able to remember what she or he is being punished for, unless the "judge" rattles off a whole lifetime-worth of errors and omission (or unless the person's memory of his life is magically restored on judgment day). The whole thing does not really make a lot of sense. It is a good story to help coerce people into behaving decently during life, and the threat of punishment by "eternal damnation" can be a very potent one. But that only works if the person accepts the dogma of that religion, and even then the threat of punishment often has little or no impact on a true and lasting change in attitude.

The concept of having only one life to experi- ence is rather depressing. There are extremely few (if any) people who have lived an exemplary life and therefore will escape judgment and punish- ment. The rest of us get one kick at the can, and then have to suffer the consequences on judgment day. We can of course pretend to avoid judgment by not believing in it, but if that day truly exists, those people are just fooling themselves until the day comes when they find out that judgment will happen anyway.

Buddhism takes a much more positive approach, and states that those fundamental "qualities" (karma) of one's life remain and will re-appear in a future life (reincarnation) during which there will be new opportunities to correct the negative actions, thoughts, emotions, and their impact on others, as experienced in previous lives

So do not despair! Buddhism offers more than just "one kick at the can", we can "repeat" our past lives and have yet more opportunities to change our life qualities from negative and harmful ones to positive ones: kindness, love, compassion, being supportive, modelling positive qualities, and many more.

If this is indeed the purpose (not the meaning) of life, then the concept of judgment day is sim- ply unnecessary. Continue to try and improve the qualities of your life experiences until you arrive at a level of perfection and inner peace that eliminates the necessity of suffering in continuing physical lives. You have then "earned" your ticket out of samsara and to "heaven"!

Meditation is an excellent tool in this quest. When one learns to observe oneself in an objective nonjudgmental manner, one begins to see more clearly one's faults and weaknesses, and also begins to discern the tools that are needed to make the necessary changes: awareness, clear thought, clear insight, clear wisdom, and loving and compassionate action.

* * *

Any major events, happy or unhappy, never happen by accident. If you believe that God (by whatever name you know Him or Her) or fate, or bad luck, has given you cancer, "It" must have had a very good reason for giving you that. If that were not the case the entire world would by now have cancer.

Those reasons can best be summarized as opportunities to learn. Perhaps you are ready at this time in your life to learn the next "lesson", that a benevolent God, or fate, or universe, or whatever you want to call it, feels that it is time for you to learn, and that *you are capable of, and entirely responsible for, leading your own life*.

So what lessons are we talking about? For me that lesson was that I must become fully and entirely responsible for my behaviours and the choices I am making in my life. If I want to be depressed, then so be it. If I don't want to be depressed, then I must take a really close look at what it is that tends to make me lean in that direction, and start making changes. The same goes for anger, fear, and all sorts of negative moods and behaviours in everyday life situations.

Am I now a perfect person? No, I am not. But I have become more aware of the choices I am making in my life, and how I can change those choices to what makes me more loving, compassionate, and happy. Those qualities do not require perfection - they require awareness, willingness to make changes, and the self-discipline to manifest and practise love and compassion.

In this context it makes no fundamental difference whether you accept the teachings of Allah, or of the Christian God, or of Brahman, or the Buddha, or the Universe, or whichever you have chosen. Whether you believe that you have, or do not have, the power and the willingness to make changes in your life, *that* does make a fundamental difference in your life. That does not negate or affect your religious beliefs; rather, they augment your worship focus by "cleaning up your act" and your life and dedicating it to serve others. And that, by the way, is my personal definition of "worship".

Dr. Carl Jung, the famous 20th century psychiatrist and philosopher, labelled this "Individuation": becoming a whole person by becoming fully aware of all aspects of oneself; both the positive and the negative ones, including the awareness of these in all their forms in daily life. This means that one needs to become fully aware of the fact that negatives are part of human nature, (dog eat dog, etc.) and that they can be disciplined or ameliorated by being completely aware of them and thereby denying them the power to affect one's life. Dr. Jung defined this process of self-realization as follows:

"the purpose of individuation is not perfection but completeness."[25]

But there is more to it than that. In order to attain individuation without fear of the results of the negatives, remember that "where attention goes, energy flows". The more one occupies one's mind with all of one's mistakes and shortcomings, the more powerful they become. This in turn focuses one's mind even more on one's faults, and that easily can become a self-energizing vicious circle that may end in serious depression.

Happily the reverse is also true: where attention is absent, energies diminish and eventually disappear completely, leaving only a residue of neutral memories of one's faults and shortcomings. Shift your attention away from the negatives and you will become a more positive, and thereby happier person! How to actually do that shifting of your attention we'll address in the following chapters.

In my own life I have through that "visitation" in that hospital solarium realized that there *is* life after death, and I have since learned that I am far from alone in that experience. It has also shown me that those who do not live in a physical body have "abilities" of which we human beings have little or no knowledge. And we know that these non-physical beings exhibit a benevolent inclination which they are willing and able to use from time to time, although we have no knowledge of under what circumstances they use those, and we can only assume that they have the wisdom to know when and how to use it.

These beings are perhaps the "saints" or "angels" who have learned their life lessons to the point where they no longer need a physical body to experience life. Perhaps they continue in a non-physical reality to learn other lessons of which we have no knowledge. In Buddhism those who have "graduated" from physical life and now devote their existence to helping others to achieve that same goal are called Bodhisattvas - perfected beings committed to supporting and teaching others.

18. Thinking Outside the Box.

Most of us live in a "box", consisting of the rules and regulations that our culture, government, religion, morals, ethics, and values place on us. We accept these because they have become our reality, and the positive ones make society safer, more secure, easier, and pleasant.

. . . and more challenging at the same time. When those rules and regulations become too suffocating or outdated we want to change them or, if that isn't happening or not fast or appropriately enough, we rebel.

Fair enough, this is one way in which our culture and society evolve, either democratically or with the application of power. Rigid societies tend to be conformist and controlling, and one section of a society may attempt to force its beliefs or opinions on others. Rigidity generally discourages independent thinking and promotes sameness.

Over the centuries creative/progressive thinkers who lived in a rigid society have paid the price: condemnation, persecution, banishment, or even death. For example, Galileo had to publicly deny his conviction that the earth circles the sun and is not the centre of the universe as the church of the day held as the ultimate truth. Not to mention the horrors of the Inquisition..

Creative thinking, thinking "outside the box", is not the same as having strong opinions, which may be a point of view, judgment, or be based on insufficient or faulty knowledge, rather than on clear and carefully evaluated facts, knowledge, and questioning. Thinking outside the box is the ability to imagine or invent something original. It is the ability to:

- generate and play with new ideas, and carefully collect and evaluate information and facts.
- investigate, change, and carefully think issues through,
- suspend judgment,
- trust intuition,
- think associatively, combine ideas
- investigate whether accepted beliefs and conclusions are true and not based on wishful thinking or ungrounded beliefs.

In addition, original thinkers need to have two special qualities:

1. Have lots of patience. Galileo's ideas were correct but it took several generations before they were generally accepted. Today there are no people left who seriously think that the earth is at the centre of the universe, but it took a while!

2. Be willing to pay the price for being controversial, from being laughed at or ostracized, and worse. Galileo was convicted to house arrest for the rest of

his life; Nelson Mandela spent 26 years in jail for his conviction that apartheid is wrong and should be abolished. He now is an international role model!

It is creative thinking that energizes the evolution of a culture and its societies. For a culture to remain vibrant it requires individuals who are willing and able to set themselves apart and think outside the established and sanctioned box. A culture that does not permit these out-of-the-box thinkers will suffer from moral, social, and artistic, rigidity and decay, and will eventually collapse. Let's try a few contemporary examples of short-sighted thinking:

* * *

The Canadian Senate.

In 1860, the "Fathers of the Canadian Confederation" decided on an appointed body, the Canadian Senate, which would apply "sober second thought" (sic) to new or revised legislation. It's task is to act as a non-ideological review body to make recommendations for new legislation, and detect errors and flaws in new or changes in current legislation.

There has now been a movement afoot to abolish the Canadian Senate, because it consist of political appointees rather then elected senators, and lately because of financial misconduct by certain senators. The prime minister (the de facto Canadian head of state) has the sole power to appoint new senators, and it has become the custom to mostly appoint stalwarts of the ruling political party. In fact the present prime minister said recently that he is pleased that his party now holds a majority of seats in the Senate so that new legislation can be "approved "expeditiously.

If the Senate no longer fulfills its mandate, should we then just abolish it? Public debate is now divided between traditionalists who say "keep the thing", and others who say "get rid of it". Yet others want to make it a democratically elected body, perhaps not fully realizing that the political partisanship and infighting in the House of Commons at times very much needs that sober second thought. No other alternatives have been proposed.

Canada has a number of highly regarded and respected citizens in the worlds of business, academia, the arts, and other endeavours, who have a lot of solid education, life experience, and practical experience in their fields of endeavour. Best of all, at least some of them no longer have a need to build their careers, prove their abilities, make their fortunes, and please their egos. Some have learned to think independently and objectively, and know how to reach consensus in difficult situations. Quite a few have been recognized for their special abilities and gifts, and by receiving the Order of Canada.

Would it be possible to charter some of these women and men to become members of a renewed Senate that can indeed provide the "sober second thought" that the Canadian Constitution requires, and the country needs rather badly? Do we perhaps need a "Council of Elders" instead of a Senate?

Not democratic - not elected, some will exclaim! The answer to such objections can be relatively simple: it can be made legal for every Canadian citizen to *nominate* a person to become a senator/elder. Of course standards will be needed so that some popular personality or the local town drunk would not be nominated as a joke. New senators/elders can then be selected by the existing Council of Elders as needed. It will take study and work to develop a workable set of qualifications and procedures, but a Senate of Elders can become an institution that indeed will introduce balance into the current political framework, and earn the respect and support of all Canadians.

A thought outside the box:

Can we develop a workable and healthy functioning system such as a Council of Elders that can contribute "Sober Second Thought," based on mature wisdom and the absence of political influences and personal agendas, and contribute toward political and societal stability?

* * *

Job Exports.

Another factory has been closed, production has been moved to a third world country, and 5,000 workers have lost their jobs (according to yesterday's news cast). The reason: lower wages in under-developed countries mean more competitive pricing and higher profits for the corporation and its shareholders..

This action does not take into account the dev-astating financial and psychological impact on the workers and their families. After all, that is "not the responsibility of the company". Neither does com-pany responsibility include the irreversible cost that exporting jobs causes to the national economy, and the cost of transferring the income of laid-off work-ers from salary-paying corporations to taxpayer-sup-ported government employment insurance resources.

There presently seem to be little or no govern-ment requirements that hold corporations respon-sible for the financial, environmental, economic, community, and individual damage they are causing in their pursuit of competitiveness and maximizing profitability. The same applies to situations where (human) workers are replaced by computers in order to maximize profitability

A thought outside the box:

Do we need legislation that prohibits, or puts severe penalties on job exports? Or alternatively, should there be import duties, payable by the cor-poration, on items previously manufactured at home but now manufactured abroad? This would also put a damper on certain corporations that state publicly that, unless the government is willing to subsidize them, they will move their plants to another coun-try. (Isn't that usually called extortion?)

Can a legal mechanism be developed (see Appendix E) to help workers find a reasonable measure of influence over job exports? Can this be achieved for example by giving workers the legal right and access to financial resources to buy company shares en masse, thereby perhaps converting a corporation into a worker-owned cooperative?

* * *

Social Responsibility.

Consider the following quotations:

"A corporation can be define[d] as a legal entity or structure created under authority of the laws of a state, consisting of a person or group of persons who become shareholders.

The simplest definition of a shareholder seems straightforward enough: an individual, institution, firm, or other entity that owns shares in a company. Corporations are only accountable to shareholders. They do not have social responsibilities.

Corporate social responsibility refers to the general belief held by growing numbers of citizens that modern business have responsibilities to society that extend beyond their obligations to the shareholders or investors in the firm."

Rephrasing the topic, it basically means that a corporation is only answerable to its shareholders, and they are not responsible for all the actions they take in order to achieve corporate goals."

Corporations not only owe their duties to the shareholders; corporations should have social responsibilities towards their actions." [26]

** Notice the use of the word "should" rather than "must".

Do corporations have any responsibilities beyond trying to maximize stockholder dividends, adhering to contracts, implicit or explicit, and obeying the laws of the different countries where they operate? The answer is "no".

Reference to the behaviour of corporations really means the behaviour of senior management who are in essence employed by stockholders through their representative boards of directors. In most cases, it is rather obvious that management must try to increase dividends through their pricing policies, the products they offer, product quality, where they locate plants, and so forth. CEO's who fail to do this are subject to termination either through takeovers or by being fired.[27] The present incestuous relationship between the corporation, represented by its senior executives, and shareholders, can best be described as "you make more money for us, we pay more money (bonuses) to you"

* * *

Acceptable behaviour of individuals within a society has long ago been defined and this accept-ability changes as a society's code of ethics evolves. Unacceptable behaviour is controlled by legislation and can result in punishment. This is not an effective way of dealing with unacceptable behaviour but, in the absence of personal self-discipline, it is the best society has been able to come up with. Perhaps the time has come to add a Bill of Responsibilities to the Canadian Bill of Right

No such Bill of Rights and Responsibilities cur-rently exists for corporations and governments. Uncontrolled cruel and excessively suppressive dic-tatorships are often condemned, and at times limits are placed on them through the use of economic or military intervention. Unfortunately even these excessive dictatorships sometimes continue to be supported for the sake of economic advantage, and some corporations use these dictatorships for the purpose of increasing their own successes.

It appears that, in addition to questionable shareholder-CEO relationships, an incestuous rela-tionship also exists between governments, political parties, and certain corporations and other organi-zations, as indicated by sometimes massive direct or indirect election campaign funding. Is this perhaps an example of the old saying that "he who pays the piper calls the tune"?

A thought outside the box:

Has the time come for society to consider the ethics of excessive corporate behaviour?

How do we address these relationships and place limitations on them without infringing on the legitimate rights of corporations and shareholders? How can this topic become the focus of a public debate? How can meaningful change be achieved, recognizing that attempts to *control* behaviour of corporations and their supporting governments will be ineffective? Is it time that a "Bill of Rights and Responsibilities" is developed to delineate unethical behaviour of corporations, their supporting governments, and individuals? Should the sometimes entirely shareholder-focused behaviours of some corporations be limited? Should this be a Canadian or an international bill"?

If this sounds like a total impossibility, consider the following European legislation:

The government of The Netherlands has approved the following declaration defining the conduct of all bankers in the country, including branches of foreign banks. The wording reflects the minimum requirements of the moral and ethical conduct of all Dutch bankers:

"I declare that I will perform my duties as a banker with integrity and care. I will carefully consider all the interests involved in the bank, i.e. those of the clients, the shareholders, the employees and the society in which the bank operates. I will give paramount importance to the client's interests and inform the

client to the best of my ability. I will comply with the laws, regulations and codes of conduct applicable to me as a banker. I will observe secrecy in respect of matters entrusted to me. I will not abuse my banking knowledge. I will act in an open and assessable manner and I know my responsibility towards society. I will endeavour to maintain and promote confidence in the banking sector. In this way, I will uphold the reputation of the banking profession."

For detailed information visit:http://www.nvb.nl/en/publications/1625/banking-code.html"

* * *

Corporations and happiness?

Am I just a dreamer with my out-of-the-box examples? Am I completely out to lunch with these unrealistic ideas? Let's look at one more example:

Bhutan is a small country of about 15,000 square miles with a population of around 750,000 people. It is bordered by China and India. Its government changed from an absolute to a constitutional monarchy, and held its first general elections in 2008. Its primary religions are Buddhism and Hinduism.

The present king, Jigme Singye Wangchuck, proposed that the country measure its progress through a "Gross National Happiness" indicator (GNH), rather than the generally accepted Gross Domestic Product" (GDP). The underlying philosophy is that economic activity and growth do not by itself produce the happiness of the Bhutanese, and that the general happiness of the population forms the basis of a healthy economy and lifestyle.

This does not mean that Bhutan does not have its problems to deal with. For example, domestic violence and persecution of minorities is still condoned by many in Bhutan.

On the other hand, it is worth noting that many Bhutanese who study abroad still prefer to return home, although wages and salaries in Bhutan are considerably lower than outside the country.

Overall it is fair to conclude that measuring the quality of life through happiness *in addition to* economic factors is an out-of-the-box idea for us westerners. But it works! Keep the example of tiny Bhutan in mind. Perhaps these off-the-wall idealistic dreams and ideas may not be all that far out of the box .

* * *

19. If You Teach your Children . . .

**If we teach our children to be consumers,
they will consume each other.
If we teach our children values,
they will value each other.**

After emigrating from Holland we arrived in our new home town of Calgary, AB. on Saturday, May 25th, 1957. On Monday morning I went downtown to the Unemployment Office, (as it was then called) and on Wednesday morning I started my first job in Canada as a stockroom clerk at a car dealership.

My salary was $200.00 per month, and with these riches we rented a one bedroom apartment with a nice view over the city for $70.00 per month. Utilities were about $ 25.00. Two years later we had saved enough money for a small down-payment on our very own house! We felt very fortunate, secure, and happy . . .

In contrast, today the 20 year old son of one of my friends is still living with his parents after graduating from high school, because he has been unable to find any job. He feels betrayed, angry, insecure, and worried about the future.

What has changed between 1957 and 2014 - in less than two generation? It is surprisingly difficult to quantify those changes because they mostly happened gradually. There were specific highlighting moments of course, the Beatles, Woodstock, and the San Francisco riots, to name but a few.

One thing that fundamentally changed was our notion of freedom. When we arrived in Calgary in 1957 we felt free, I had an instant starter job, we could save money to buy our first home, and we were already talking about starting a family. To my wife and I, that was real freedom, compared to the over-crowding and housing shortages in post-war Holland.

But those simple freedoms began to change from freedom to act within the values of society, to "freedom to do whatever you want". In the 1970's credit cards began to appear and soon added "do what you want, buy what you want, and buy it *when* you want". But freedom without discipline is merely egocentricity. At this point in time rapidly increasing greed entered daily life and, as an almost unavoidable result, the focus on money and attachment to getting more and more "things" accelerated. A nearly unlimited consumer society had been created.

This is the set of values that young people today are growing up with; a feeling of entitlement is what has become their reality. These same people are now not only today's consumers; they are or will be the business owners and corporation CEO's who shape their businesses within that value system of gaining power and control, of manipulating the market and *making* money rather than earning it.

Have we really grown beyond the age-old drives of competition and domination?

* * *

If we really are happy with all that new-found freedom, why has the divorce rate skyrocketed to nearly 50% of all marriages? How long does that new fancy car stay "new"? How different are we from the old Roman empire: bread and games for the people - government by the elite. That was a policy that worked well . . . until that empire collapsed because of degenerating values and morals.

Can we avoid a similar fate? Can we achieve change? Can basic human drives be modified despite the rigidity of basic human nature? And if so, how?

Joining a political party will be of very little help. All parties seem to feel that it is their task to criticize their opponents, (not to mention the near-violent confrontational attitudes during certain elections) and must raise money to finance their next election campaign. "He who pays the piper still calls the tune."

Passing more laws and regulations does not work well either. Human behaviour cannot be changed by attempts to control it. Helping to alleviate many forms of distress by joining a non-profit service-oriented society is a good step, but it cannot achieve a broadly based change in values and ethics. What can we do?

* * *

The time to attempt lasting change is when behaviours and values are *formed*, and before they become firmly established. It is before they have become a person's inner reality. That period is during the time of gestation and early childhood, Children do as their parents do; not as their parents say!

- Can we explain and demonstrate to kids how parents' values and behaviours become their children's values and behaviours?

- Can we teach children how to act when they themselves become parents?

- Can we explain in simple terms how existential distortion works to protect kids from getting carried away by their emerging sexual drives?

- Can we explain to children the principles and purpose of religion and spirituality? Perhaps the contemporary purpose of religion can be defined as: to create harmony, develop kindness, compassion, and community at all levels.

- There is a billboard near downtown, depicting a mother and child, that reads "read to your child, and read often". Perhaps one could add "Sing with your child, and sing often".

- Can we explain in simple terms the basic concept of dependent origination to help children understand the temporary nature of all goods and curb excessive materialism?

- Start a small garden with your child, explain in simple terms how life evolves from seed to flower to seed, and how care for all living things is part of living compassionately.

- Wouldn't it be wonderful if a cooperative could be formed to promote wholesome children's entertainment on television. (What happened to Mr. Dress-up and Dr. Seuss?). Meanwhile choose the right programs for kids and block the rest.

- Expose your child to art. In most cities and towns there are free art exhibitions in museums and galleries; take your child to music performances but avoid heavy beat and excessively loud music (can cause hearing damage too)

- School gardens teach creativity, cooperation, and where the food one eats comes from.

- Broaden children's understanding of life and its values with art activities, creative dance, visit a symphony orchestra with wide spaces between the rows of musicians so that kids can walk around, see musicians at work, and ask questions; visit a pop musician who is writing a new song and ask the kids to make suggestions; talk with and see visual artists, sculptors, and dancers at work.

- Form debating clubs. This teaches kids that there are often several valid but different perceptions (not answers or opinions, and please explain the difference) of a given topic and that black-and-white answers are often little more than poorly considered opinions. It also teaches public speaking, thinking on their feet, using appropriate and clear language, and becoming more aware of their own feelings and those of others.

- Community service for kids: create opportunities to visit elderly persons, volunteer at a multi-cultural centre or a hospital, etc.

- Corp. or co-op? Emphasize the difference between a corporation and a cooperative, what cooperative community really means, and explain the basics of how the economy and politics of a country work, the pro's and con's of different structures, and their ethical implications.

- Teach an understanding of what has shaped today's society and culture; what were the causes that led to 20th century wars, investigate major societal changes such as the industrial revolution, the cultural revolution in China, the North American evolution of freedom, and ask kids what the values of a healthy caring society should consist of.

- Teach objective thinking, and explain "perception". What matters is not what a person believes but how she/he arrives at his/her beliefs.

- Set up drop-in centres for adolescents where elders in the community can play an important role: be available to listen and, when asked for, offer and explain suggestions and alternatives to young people.

* * *

These are just some examples of how we can make a start with creating and incorporating a value set for our younger people. Many parts of this must be included in the basic curriculum of all schools: on how a decent, caring, compassionate society can function; where values are recognized by young people as being in their own and their society's best interest.

Would it not be wonderful if a national conference could be organized to discuss these and many other ideas, and where knowledgeable speakers are invited to present new ideas, and start and moderate discussions?

Who can afford to live without beauty?

Beauty fills us with passion;

it graces us with joy and lights up our existence.

A landscape, a piece of music, a film, a dance -

Suddenly all the dreariness is gone,

we are left bewitched, we are dazzled.

If we get lost in dark despair,

beauty takes us back to Centre. [28]

**   *   ***

20. Giving yourself away.

The limitations of language can cause curious issues that may be difficult to resolve. Take the English word "love" for example. In classical Greek there are four words for love: eros, philia, storge, and agape; English has only one commonly used word.

Eros Is of course physical, passionate love, experienced as longing and sensual desire. Eros relates directly to the sexual instinct, and as such consist of powerful but relatively momentary experiences.

Philia Is the love that is much less passionate. It is the love shared between family members and between friends.

Storge is a more immediate and powerful form of philia, found between parents and their children. Physical, and especially emotional storge is the foundation for true caring for your child.

And then there is agape: spiritual unconditional love, free of Eros, and surpassing philia and storge. Agape places no expectations or judgment on anyone or anything: a feeling of happy contentment that is sometimes difficult to describe and, unlike eros, philia, and storge, much more difficult to contain in words.

Note: please be aware that "amor" is not a Greek word. The god Amor was the son of the Roman goddess Venus and is also known as Cupid, which name derives from the Latin word cupido: desire. Amor represents the Roman equivalent of Eros. He is of course famous for his bow and arrows. What is noteworthy is that Amor is blindfolded, shooting his arrows indiscriminately and out of the blue, apparently looking for sex rather than for a sustainable life partner relationship.

The lack of these distinctions in the English language has some unfortunate consequences, amplified by the emphasis on eros in the media and entertainment businesses. It is not too surprising that intimate relationships that are based purely on eros fail after eros energy diminishes and turns out to have little longer-term philia and storge energy to support it.

* * *

The term "knowledge" suffers from similar indistinctiveness. "To know" means of course to have collected sufficient information to recognize, understand, and describe an object, although the depth of this knowledge can vary widely depending on the nature of the object.

An inanimate object is known primarily by its appearance and what it consists of. A rock can be smooth or coarse, heavy or light, light or dark in colour, sandstone or granite, and so forth.

The sciences strive to add further dimensions to knowledge through gaining a much more detailed understanding of physical matter by combining, manipulating. and studying matter. Without these studies we would still largely be living the life of hunter-gatherers. In order to be accepted as valid, scientific knowledge must be able to:

- formulate a valid rational explanation of phenomena and processes,

- demonstrate the same results and conclusions repeatedly.

- where appropriate, express findings and conclusions mathematically.

All living beings can be known by properties that are similar to those described for matter: hair/fur and eye colour, skin texture, build, posture, means of locomotion, etc., as well as instinctual drives, behaviours, and what animals learn during their life time. Some species appear to have a consciousness that indicates memory, affection, bonding, etc. But for more evolved beings we can add an additional dimension: *individual* "qualities" such as individual aggression or passivity, competitiveness or friendliness, kindness or anger, compassion or egocentricity, love or hate, inquisitiveness, experimentation, spirituality, philosophical thinking, and many more. In short, a host of behaviours and qualities that stem directly or indirectly from the fundamental drives that we already observed in chapter 6:

- ☐ survival   - eat and be eaten,
- ☐ reproduction - the continuation of the species;
- ☐ power   - social / gender dominance,
- ☐ competition - between individuals, clans, and tribes

If these *instinctual drives* constitute the fundamental nature of humanity, they cannot be changed or eliminated, although the resulting *behaviours* can be modified. Secondly, one needs to know all of the developed and undeveloped resources and the circumstances that influence these behaviours.

But if the instinctual nature of humanity cannot be changed, then what is the use of describing them yet again? Let us take a look at a few examples of a resource that has remained largely undeveloped in contemporary Western society but has the power to moderate the effects of these instinctual drives: a different form of "knowing". Here are a few examples:

1. In Chapter 3 we talked already about the mysterious appearance in that hospital solarium, followed three days later by that strange conflict between the cancerous biopsy sample and the benign surgery results.

Not terribly scientific of course: no experiments, it cannot be repeated reliably in a similar manner and it cannot be mathematically described. But there were several reliable witnesses and the results were irrefutable. But I "know" exactly what happened. All I had to do was connect the dots so to speak, by linking my solarium "visitor" to the baffling surgery results.

2. Here is a second different and more "definable" example: that beautiful line, set to such inspiring music by Georg Friederick Handel in *the Messiah*: "I know that my Redeemer liveth". How did Handel "know" that, never having met his Redeemer in person? By mouthing biblical texts to please his devout audience; by experiencing his faith? Listen to his music and you too will "know" the answer.

Is there something we should perhaps call "experiential knowing" (for want of a better term) that is an "inner" and very personal experience, as subjective as it may be? One that transcends all but would never pass the scientific validity tests? Many examples can be found in the works of truly inspired poets like Rumi, and of musicians, artists, and of the teachers and saints of the Muslim, Hindu, Buddhists, Christian, and other religions and spiritual traditions.

3. Here is a different example. I already briefly mentioned in chapter 10 the experiences when I sit vigils with dying persons. These vigils end of course when the person passes away. What happens before that moment is difficult to describe because English and other languages have no words for it, and the common metaphors are usually rather uninformative.

When a dying person is still able to communicate we may already have talked about topics such as the meaning of life, death and dying, fears about judgment, about mistakes made and opportunities missed. And sometimes I may sense an unresolved issue or unanswered question, and very gently reflect on that during the person's final days or hours.

Especially when a dying person is in a coma or otherwise unable to communicate, it is imperative that I maintain physical contact with that person: hold her hand or put my hand on her arm or forehead and reassure her: "I am with you in this, dear . . ." The purpose is to maintain physical contact with the dying person so that she or he does not feel alone or abandoned, and experiences unnecessary fear of the upcoming unknown. And then there are moments when I know intuitively that the dying person needs to rest or have silent time to meditate or pray and prepare him/herself for the next stage to come.

But, you may ask, how do I know about those unresolved issues when the person is in a coma? I sense it because I seem to enter a different "space". Literally everything falls away: my surroundings, sounds and images, my own worries and fears, and even my ego seems to take a back seat. It feels like I literally become empty (oh, those lame metaphors), and become completely open to the other person. We become directly connected and communicate wordlessly and without having to "think". We'll come back to this later in this chapter.

* * *

Let's investigate what this space consist of. You will need a few sheets of 8.5 x 11" unlined white paper like computer printing paper, a medium ball-point pen, a coloured highlighter pen, a ruler, and a glue stick or sticky tape.

1. On a sheet of paper either glue a passport-size picture of yourself in profile, sitting on a straight chair in front of a plain wall, or make a 2" x 3" sketch of yourself in that position. It doesn't matter whether you sit straight or slouch, legs crossed or feet on the floor, where your arms and hands are, and whether it is a good or bad image of yourself, as long as you recognize it as being yourself. Then draw a number of 3" lines radiating out from the edges of the picture or sketch, with arrow points at the ends of the lines. Then write across the top of the sheet "How others see me".

Write at the end of each arrow a word that expresses a quality of yourself as you imagine *others see you*. These can be positive or negative, such as gentle or angry, friendly of unfriendly, generous or stingy, considerate or selfish, accepting or judgmen-tal, etc. Take lots of time and don't judge yourself. Try and be as honest as you can and remember that this is only as *others* perceive you.

Question: does this describe the *real* you? Is this the way you really are?

2. Now glue another picture or make a sketch (same size) in the centre of a second sheet of paper. This should be just a head and shoulders picture like a

passport or driver's license photo. Write across the top of the sheet "The way I see myself", and again draw radiating lines but this time with the arrows pointing inward.

Next, at the outside ends of the lines, write words that describe how you see *yourself*. It's OK to boast or to judge yourself, as long as you use words that describe *how you feel about yourself*. Please take lots of time for this and remember that this is private information that you will never be asked to share with anyone else.

Questions:
- is this the *real* you; the way you really are?

- do you like yourself this way? If this description of yourself is very positive you are likely to be a very happy person; if it is very negative it is not likely that you lead a very happy life. But whichever it is, there may also be sides of you that you haven't yet explored.

- with the highlighter pen, highlight the words on *both* previous sheets that describe the kind of person you would *like* to be. Don't be modest - simply be straightforward about your ideals.

- once you have described the person you would like to be, write down useful practical ways or methods that you can use to implement these goals.

While exploring those potential useful practical ways and methods, you may soon discover that your inborn instincts stand in the way of success. As long as you struggle with issues of survival, reproduction, power, and dominance, and all the thoughts, feelings, and behaviours that flow from those, becoming the person you would like to be will likely elude you. But if there is no way to eliminate these instincts, is humanity then doomed to continue living in a world filled with daily violence? Is there no way out; do we have no choice but to remain caught in that vicious circle of uncontrollable instincts? And where do we find that "way out", and what would that consist of?

First of all, remember Chapter 12: "Where attention goes, energy flows". If for example you watch a lot of violence on TV (the news, violence in movies, etc.), or have experienced a trauma such as a serious accident, violence such as wartime experiences, or a life-threatening illness, your increasing stress levels will reinforce the kind of person you may *not* want to be, aggravated by illnesses such as post-traumatic stress disorder, fear and anxiety or depression. You may not be consciously aware of that stress increase as it becomes the way you experience your daily life, but it may eventually affect your physical and mental health, and your daily behaviours. On the other hand, if you consciously focus your attention on positive and happy life experiences, that is where your energies will flow to and improve your physical, emotional, and spiritual health. That is not to say that you should ignore negatives or push it under the carpet. Acknowledge them but don't allow these to become a strong focus of your attention. They are what they are, and judging them as "bad" does not make them better or send them away. That judgment may well mess up your life.

So how do we focus on positives in a negative or painful environment? That is where a "different kind of knowing" can pay great dividends. Read on . .

3. In the centre of a third sheet of paper draw a 3"x4" horizontal rectangle with three 2" lines radi- ating at a moderate upward angle from the left- hand bottom and top corners and from the right hand top corner, plus a fourth *dotted* line from the right bottom corner (in the same direction).

Connect the end of the line from the left top corner to the ends of the lines from the left bot- tom and right top corner. Connect the end of the fourth (dotted) line to the lines merging from the left bottom and right top corner with dotted lines. The drawing will now represent a see-through three dimensional object like a brick or a box.

In the left side panel of the "box" write the word "Agape"; in the top panel the word "Compassion", in the right hand panel write "Gratitude", and in the front panel write "Acceptance". Then, at the top of the sheet write "My Equanimity Space"

Agape is an acknowledgment or expression of unconditional, non-judgmental love toward self and another person or group of people.

Acceptance is the respectful acknowledgment of a person(s) as he or she is, without judging any differences in race, gender, beliefs, appearance, qualities or other characteristics.

Compassion is a mind set from which flows the practical expression of acceptance and offering of agape love to the pain and suffering of others.

Gratitude is a calm and balanced acceptance and appreciation of whatever comes your way, regardless of its values or its utility, and whether it is pleasant or unpleasant.

Equanimity is a mind set that indicates perfect composure: a way of being when all positive and negative energies are in balance. Notice that this definition indicates the presence of both positives *and* negatives, rather than the absence of negative energies. Equanimity therefore does not require perfection.

You may want to find or make an actual box, make it your Equanimity Box, and write the same four words on its sides. Then write your choices of the words you chose for your life on strips of paper and put them in the box. You may want to go back to take another look at them later on and perhaps add a few more to the box. If you like, you can also strips of paper with the words that describe how you do *not* want to be, and remove those from the box when you feel you've got a handle on those.

Equanimity can be achieved by choosing to focus your attention on the contents of the Equanimity Box, rather than feel overpowered by a world full of violence, suffering and struggle. It may also be helpful to phrase those equanimity words into a mantra, to be repeated as often as you wish. For example, you could use a mantra such as "today I will be kind, happy, and healthy". Feel free to invent your own mantra!

Focusing on positives rather than on negative conditions and feelings is not the same as ignoring or denying them. Instead, focusing on equanimity means contributing positive energies to the world around you. This is perhaps only a miniscule contribution at first, but when using this kind of mantras becomes "viral" it will indeed change the world into a better place - one step at the time

* * *

We are already experiencing a new era of unbridled individual freedom, not only in traditional Western civilizations but also in Africa, the Middle East and across Asia. Unfortunately those freedoms are at times earned through violent confrontations, and stability may not yet have been reached as renewed competition for power and control erupt again. Freedom without restraint seems almost invariably to result in chaos.

Why does freedoms not result in a better world? It is because freedom requires self-discipline (not externally-imposed discipline). Self-discipline is a personal quality, not something one can learn from a book or from attending a few seminars and work-shops, although those may at times be helpful. The awareness and insights that foster self-discipline must be learned in early childhood from the exam-ples of one's elders, and at times it can also be the result of experiencing trauma. And that awareness in turn requires both insight into, and the experi-ence of, that reality of equanimity.

I have sensed an eagerness, especially among the younger generation, for fundamental changes, and have heard many comments that: "we cannot continue in this old way any longer; mass murder by so-called governments, mass surveillance in the electronic world, and organized crime and inter-net bullying *must* stop." I foresee that before the end of the 21st century powerful confrontations will develop between huge neo-capitalist multi-national corporations and their supporting govern-ments, (impersonal and computer driven as they are) and respect and freedom seeking individuals who will be energized by a vision of a very differ-ent world, and by their quest for disciplined true freedom.

* * *

Let us now return for a moment to the comment made earlier in this chapter: "I seem to enter a dif-ferent space". This is not an other-worldly or super-natural space. It is in fact the Equanimity Space we have discussed above: a space where all positive and negative energies, including the ego, are in bal-ance and require little attention, leaving one free to focus completely on the other person: on relief from suffering, and on attaining peace and happiness.

By publicly sharing a few of my intimately personal experiences, it is my hope that you may come to recognize and "know" this experiential reality of equanimity that may contain the seeds of a compassionate society. What that society will look like the future will tell, but I share Dr. Turok's quote shown at the end of Chapter 10, *"We are being challenged to the next level of existence, the next stage in the evolution of ourselves and of the universe."*

To summarize: I have learned over the past 30 years that the only way towards progress is to open my heart. Hence the title of this chapter: "Giving yourself away" (cf. Appendix C). In a very real sense, giving myself way, no longer needing my individuality, is the spirit of equanimity: stepping beyond my grasping little ego and undisciplined thoughts, and reaching for the sacred space of equanimity. Sharing that is ultimately the purpose of writing this book.

As Jonathan Livingston Seagull said a few decades ago:
    "It is good to be a seeker,

    But one day you have to become a Finder.

    And then it is good to share what you have found

    With those who are willing to receive."

Epilogue.

It has been a pleasure to share these thoughts and discoveries with you.

The story of the Coffee Maker is the story of evolving humanity. For all of us who in some way are wandering around in that great dark forest of ignorance and instinctual drives I say: stay open to that tiny event, that little white rabbit or whatever it happens to be for you. If you are not alert to that, that tiny rabbit may take the form of a dragon as it did for me: a very close brush with death from cancer. If I had been more alert, that may not have happened.

Be ever alert for Bodhisattvas or guardian angels, or whatever they are supposed to be called. They tend to show up in the most unlikely places! They are our teachers and guides, and we owe them great respect and gratitude for their knowledge, wisdom, and compassion.

Where am I now in that story of life? Thanks to cancer I found my way out of the forest and shared many a cup of "coffee" with Mr. C., a composite of my several mentors. Thanks to a pretty bad experience with existential distortion, I found that "town with a tiny market place and a vacant little shop", where I found all the ingredients I needed to manifest that magic coffee machine. And what does that coffee maker look like? It looks like nothing you have ever seen because it is invisible and consists entirely of gold-materialized compassion. I am filled with gratitude for the many teachings I have received, and for the many opportunities I have had and still receive to attempt to practise my beliefs.

This is of course anything but the end of the story. Sometimes I think that I have found it when I forget myself for a moment and "give myself away" to someone else. And then I forget all about it again in my busyness of daily life and relapse into my ordinary every-day self. But the results of the magic moments are invariably filled with grace when I see a person change from a man or woman who is wandering around in his or her dark forest into someone who all of a sudden can look into the whole wide world and start making choices in what he or she wants to find there. The options are really unlimited, and the results are true miracles, even as tiny as they sometimes seem to be.

That elusive meaning of life has nothing to do with what you do. You will find it in what you *are*. I invite each and every one of you who have read this book to become a little more vulnerable, to open your heart, watch for little white rabbits, and encounter a world full of opportunities for learning and service.

* * *

Let's accept that we are all one; that we cannot know what Life is until we have learned to think in terms of energies rather than in terms of measurable physicality or religiosity. Life Energy is not the body, nor is it the emotions or the mind. Neither is it physics or religion. Life Energy is what it is, and we may never find the answer to what its true nature is. It may also turn out that the life energy is dependent on a preceding cause or process, but as yet we have no knowledge of that at all. The only thing we may learn is that this Life Energy is at the core — the very existence — of everything alive in the universe, on earth, on the stars and, who knows, in other realities. Once we learn to respect this, we will finally become truly FREE . . .

In the Introduction I wrote ". . . *all of us somehow "know" that there is something bigger and better than we find in daily life*." Add to this my "discovery" that when I smile, I can feel something happening in my chest: it opens my heart chakra. I experience this as a physical feeling. When I walk down the street I habitually smile at other people, even when they avoid eye contact, and something happens.

There are those of us who are the dreamers, who never quite fit into society, and who our culture eyes with mild suspicion. These are the misfits who create that golden urn, who pour their love (rather than their mathematics) into their passion. They are the ones who prevent the human race from becoming a race of computer-driven machines and gadgets. Ultimately, they are the ones who keep us sane with their confusing insanity.

In closing I want to share with you a brief paragraph I received many years ago in a thank-you note from one of my clients. It requires no explanation:

"I have been reflecting on this silly new year's tradition of making resolutions. I came to the conclusion that every single day you are able to wake up, you have the potential of a new day in which your potential to change what is happening is only as far away as your own thoughts and actions!

That potential is limitless and your potential to be more every day is abounding in the wealth you put into that decision to make your life work and not let anyone get in the way of who you are and what you can become. It's all in your own hands, you are simply your own creator and the potential of what you can do is only bound by your limited thinking."

* * *

May the light that shines on us all

Illuminate your heart,

Bless all who cross your path.

And offer you happiness and gratitude.

* * *

Appendix A:

Meditation and Contemplation.

What is meditation?

First of all, what it is not. Meditation is not a religious exercise. It is not prayer and does not address any "higher being". In fact, meditation does not address anyone or anything except yourself.

A part of the human mind can be compared to an archive where all kinds of information about old experiences, thoughts, and feelings, are stored so that they can be retrieved in the future when needed. This explains why sometimes in the most unexpected way an old memory pops up again in your mind. A déjà vu is a good example, something in the present reminds you of something, and triggers the memory of a previous experience. This implies that there are "communications" happening between that present aware part of the mind, and the contents of that "storage room", even if we are not consciously aware of it.

One purpose of meditation is to broaden and strengthen those channels of communication so that one becomes more able to be clearly aware of, and investigates previous memories, experiences, their "emotional charge", and the stresses these can produce.

Another purpose of meditation is to eliminate interference by our "practical" rational thinking and our "emotional mind" that tends to hinder creativity and objectivity.

Stress can be one of the factors that contribute to the start and/or progress of chronic diseases. This is something that we can address through our meditation efforts. Help from a professional counsellor or psychologist can be very valuable, but even then we ourselves can contribute effectively to those professional services.

Thus the immediate purpose of meditation is to put the mind at rest, avoid the interferences of old memories and their emotional charge, and become relaxed and peaceful.

But there is much more to it than that. The goal is not that we learn to sit without moving for an hour with a blank look in our eyes; meditation is not navel gazing! An important purpose of meditation is that we can learn to be open to looking at ourselves, our environment, and at our own personal history in a coolly objective manner; that we can see ourselves: our thoughts, our actions, our feelings and emotions, and our environment, exactly as they are without value judgment.

Can it be done? Yes, and people have been doing it for centuries. What does it take? Commitment and patience; learning to meditate is an ongoing process that may be helpful for a person with cancer and other chronic diseases.

What results to expect? That is different for every person, but in general, peace of mind, objectivity so that you are not being driven by subconscious energies, and noticeable improvement of your physical and mental well-being. Meditation by itself is not a cure for cancer, but you'll begin to feel so much better about the feelings and emotions you experience as a result of your cancer diagnosis, about the way you experience pain, and the side effects of treatments such as radiation and chemotherapy can become much less invasive and easier to deal with.

Sounds like it is worth a try? Let's start!

* * *

How to Meditate

1. **Location,**

Find a quiet place where you can sit without interruptions. Ringing phones, children wanting your attention, loud traffic noises, and the dog wanting to go outside do not help you to relax and focus.

Your room should be cool but not cold. Wear loose comfortable clothes. If it is too warm you will be tempted to doze off.

2. **Posture,**

It is advisable but not required to sit on the floor. If you are comfortable doing that, a thick but solid cushion will protect your backside from getting sore and your legs from feeling cramped.

It is not required that you sit in a lotus position with your left knee bent, holding it close to or on the floor while the top of your left foot rests on the inside of the right thigh, and then pulling the right foot on top of the left thigh, keeping the knee low.

This is good for lithe young people but murderous for us older ones. Instead you may try to sit in a half-lotus position: put your right foot onto your left thigh, and bend your left knee until your left foot touches your right knee, but don't pull your foot on top of your right thigh. You can also do that the other way around with your left foot on your right thigh etc. Try to keep both knees close to or on the floor. Again, don't strain. Relax your sitting position till you are reasonably comfortable. If you cannot comfortably do a half-lotus potion, just find a sitting position that doesn't strain your muscles. Meditation is not an exercise in making pretzels!

If your back is not up to remaining straight while sitting on the floor and your pelvis starts to sag and disturb your balance, sit on a chair instead. Use a comfortable straight-backed chair. Heavily padded furniture will tempt you to slouch and fall asleep. Be aware of:

- Putting your feet flat on the floor and do not cross your legs or ankles.

- The seat of the chair should be high enough (if you're tall) or low enough (if you're short) so that your upper legs are more or less horizontal and your knees are not much higher or lower than your pelvis.

- Sit with your bum against the back of the chair so that your back is straight with a slight curve forward at the small of your back. You should feel your tailbone touching the back of your chair.

- Tilt your head and neck slightly back so that there is a small curve backward in your neck, but do not push your chin out. Don't let your head slump forward; this will tempt you to go to sleep and may give you a feeling of depression.

- Now put your left hand in your lap, palm up. Then put your right hand, also palm up, in your left hand. Some like to put the right hand so that the palm covers the fingers of the left hand. Others prefer to cover the entire palm of the left hand with the right hand. Either way, your hands should be in an open position. It is also OK to place your hands palms up on your thighs. Your posture should signify openness.

Some people experience a slight tingling or feeling of light pressure in the palms of the upturned hands. This may give you a feeling of energy and feeling refreshed. Whether this is an awareness of an "external energy" or one's imagination I leave up to you to decide. In either case, this feeling is normal and experienced by many, and there is no reason for concern.

3. Progressive Muscle Relaxation,

After checking your posture when starting your meditation, it is useful to check that your body and all its muscles are relaxed. A quick and easy way to do that is as follows:

1. start by bringing your focus of attention to your feet, and check that all muscles there are fully relaxed. Wiggle your toes. You may want to spread your toes and move your feet sideways back and forth from the ankles.

2. let your focus of attention very slowly travel up each leg, checking that all muscles are relaxed. Do this slowly, there is no need to rush.

3. let your attention slowly travel up your back to your shoulders and then down the front of your torso. The lower back, shoulders, chest and abdomen in particular are places where there often is a lot of tension.

4. now let your attention, again slowly, travel down each arm and hand in turn, again relaxing any tension spots.

5. finally, check the muscles in your neck, a real tension spot. Check all muscles in your scalp and your face, and down to your throat. These muscles are particularly prone to holding a

lot of tension, so take plenty of time to check these locations.

Now your entire body should be in a very relaxed state. If there are still any places that hold tension, check those again.

4. Calm your mind.

Like most people, you may find that your ever-busy mind won't let you settle down. Thoughts keep flashing through your head, demanding your attention. Here are four simple ways to slow this down and eventually, after lots of practice, you will find that those thoughts will pretty much stop altogether.

a. Focus on your breath.

"Deep breathing" helps to switch your focus of attention away from your busy thoughts. When inhaling, first gently push out just your abdomen so you can take in a full breath, and then exhale slowly. Try to breathe with your abdomen only (not your chest) for a few moments.

Now push out only your chest while leaving your abs motionless. Try to only breathe this way for a bit. By combining these two ways of breathing, your chest will fill with quite a lot of air. Don't overdo it by forcing air in and out; it may make you cough or dizzy. After breathing in, hold your breath for 2 or 3 seconds and then exhale slowly. **B**reathe deeply and slowly in a relaxed manner. This kind of focus on your breathing will relax your mind and provide your system with lots of oxygen.

If your nasal passages are reasonably clear, close your mouth and breathe in through your nose. You will feel cool air moving through your nostrils, and hear air going in through your nose and throat. If your nose is congested, breathe through your mouth, observing the same effects. You can also combine both by inhaling through your nose and exhaling through your mouth. You will notice that your body soon begins to relax even more, and your shoulders may start to sag a bit.

b. Follow the flow of energies through your body.

It is said that there is a constant flow of life energy (chi) that circulates through your body. You can start at the base of your spine and let it flow up the front of your body through the chakras (refer back to chapter 16: Many Paths, One Truth.) to the top of your head. It then flows down along your spine until it arrives again at the base of your spine. You will be able to follow this flow by focusing on a feeling of slight pressure moving up the front of your body, pausing briefly at each chakra, and then down your spine. There may be places where you don't feel that "pressure", for example in your middle back which is not a very sensitive spot in your body, but that's not a problem.

Move slowly, there is no need to rush. Each circuit may take some 15 to 20 seconds, but choose a tempo that feels relaxed for you. You do not need to breath in sync with following your energies. Following a continuous circular flow is very relaxing.

c. Focusing on an image.

Focusing on an object or mental image with your eyes open or closed is a good way to distract your busy mind from all those busy thought. However sitting with your eyes open may distract you, and it may be easier to start with your eyes closed. Focus on an image that you can picture in your mind. Anything can be used as an image, but it is best to choose a neutral image; objects such as food or your new car will fire up your thoughts again. A flower, candle flame or a peaceful nature scene are calmer and easier to focus on. Remember that candle at meal time? (see page 99) Of course the image of the Buddha or a religious figure or symbol fits in well. You may also want to listen to some very quiet and calming music or nature sounds

To begin with you need to become thoroughly familiar with the object of your choice, whether it is a mental image or the real object. Look carefully at your object, its size, shape, colour, texture, etc. You will soon be able to picture it in your mind's eye. You may want to mentally surround it with light. You are of course free to experiment with different objects until you hit on one that really works for you.

d. Using a mantra.

A mantra is a brief line of words or sounds that helps to focus you. This may be recited out loud or silently. They may have a meaning and/or a religious content, but not necessarily so. Examples are

- Religious: There is only one God and Mohammad is his prophet.
- Universal: May there be peace on earth.
- Buddhist: Om Mani Padme Hum

This Buddhist mantra actually consist of six separate syllables, and is pronounced: Ohm Ma (as in machine) Ni (as in bee) Pe (as in pet) Me (as in May) Hum (as in boom)

Mantras can be sounded at a normal pace, the ones listed above usually take about 3 - 4 seconds and they can be repeated without pause, unless a pause is needed to complete a rhythmic pattern (see item "e" below).

Other mantras can be invented as desired, but all have certain qualities in common that must be observed for a mantra to be effective:

i. They are brief. Long sentences will make you think.

ii. Mantras must have a "value" or meaning rather than be just random

The examples shown above of course include something meaningful; in the Buddhist mantra the syllables have no immediately obvious meaning of their own, but are believed to contain powerful energies.

You are certainly encouraged to develop your own mantra, one that speaks directly to your personal needs and circumstances. I have developed my own mantra that suits my needs and that I use during meditation as well as during my daily activities,

"be peaceful, be kind, be happy."

As I repeat this silently I can feel a slight smile forming on my face . . .

e. Mantras have a certain rhythm. (bold indicates an accent)

1 **2**, 1 **2**, 1 **2**,   Om **Ma** Ni **Pad** Me **Hum**

1 2 3, **1** 2 3   **May** there be **peace** on earth

1 **2** 3, 1 **2** 3, 1 **2** . .   Lord **Jesus** I **Send** you my **Love** . . .

In the 3rd example the last syllable is absent and is replaced with a pause to maintain the rhythm of the mantra.

f. Their focus is non-material.

The mantra, "To - **night** I want **steak** for my **din** - ner " is focused on something you want for yourself.

If you really want to include the word "steak" in your mantra, try something like "May **all** who are **hun** - gry have **steak** for their **din**- ner", although of course this is pretty silly for a mantra !

g. The use of prayer/meditation beads can be very helpful as a focus for your mind, as well as for maintaining the rhythm of your mantra. Tibetan meditation beads have 108 beads, which is considered a meaningful number, and helps to give you a sense of how long you have been reciting your mantra. When I use Tibetan meditation beads it usually takes some 5 minutes to complete one circuit.

Please remember to recite your mantra slowly. One sometimes hears monks reciting Om Mani Padme Hum [29] quite rapidly but that is not required. Trying to relax your mind while speeding your mantra makes little sense. So choose a tempo that feels relaxed for you.

5. How long to meditate

In the beginning, a few minutes is fine. Continue as long as you feel comfortable and not agitated or stressed by interruptions or by trying to do it "right". You will gradually begin to feel comfortable, and extend your meditation time. There is a great story about Swami Muktananda where he advised someone to meditate for 5 minutes each day and add one minute per week. In one year he would be meditating for an hour a day (actually 57 minutes, but who's counting?) Don't watch the clock; observe your level of comfort and relaxation instead; you are not trying to set a world record! If you eventually can reach 30 minutes you are doing wonderful. The length of time will vary from day to day. Some days you'll be really relaxed and your meditation can easily last for a whole hour; other days you'll be squirming after 5 minutes, so stop then and there. Trust your feelings!

The most important part of meditating is that you meditate every day. A few times each day for a few minutes is better than trying for an hour once a day. If your day becomes too stressful you may want to take a couple of minutes out of your busy schedule and try deep breathing or do the progressive muscle relaxation to refresh your body and mind. Take it easy and remain relaxed; you will progress as long as you don't force it

You may find that initially your mind will invent all sorts of excuses to postpone and then skip your meditation. Those are the tricks of the human mind. Just observe these interferences as mind tricks, and try to develop a daily routine. The same time(s) every day is by far the best and easiest way to meditate. Let's not even talk about deciding on a *discipline* for meditation; the whole purpose of meditation is to relax body and mind, and put some limits on those pesky thoughts.

A final piece of advice: be gentle with yourself. The more you try to control those interrupting thoughts, the more insistent and attention-seeking they become. Remember that "where attention goes, energy flows"!

* * *

A special note for care givers.

I have been a hospice volunteer for many years, and I feel grateful for the opportunities I had to share difficult and sometimes painful parts of other peoples' lives, and at times have had the opportunity to make some meaningful contribution of support and love. I have also experienced some very powerful feelings of powerlessness, the feeling that there is so little if anything that I can really *do*. Those feelings of powerlessness are not easy to dispel, or at least put into some manageable perspective.

Keep in mind that you are not there to *do* anything for the other person. *Doing* things: running errands, house cleaning, or making meals, is not your job as a *support* person. That does not mean that you should not help out that way, but those tasks are a whole different way of offering support.

A support person is someone who is willing and able to *listen* to another person: to be understanding, refrain from any kind of judgment, and never give advice. To be fully present to someone at all times is true support: silence is golden. The ability to help a person to become relaxed and comfortable is really important, and if you have the skills to open up topics of conversation you are offering a priceless service. If for example you sense that the other person is worried about a particular thing (he or she may already have alluded to that), then try and steer the conversation gently to that topic. Listen and paraphrase statements back to the person ("I understand that you are worried about . . .").

For care givers I have found the following healing mantra to be of enormous help to maintain or regain my inner balance, to remain as objective as I can, and to keep some control over the seemingly never ending chatter of my inner voice. It goes as follows:

I am sorry,
Please forgive me,
I love you (or me).

(See further in Appendix F)

* * *

Keeping in mind the old adage that "one can lead a horse to water but cannot make him drink" leads to renewing the insight that you cannot *make* another person change. Suffering, negativity, depression, and so many other feelings that stand in the way of healing, are very strong attachments, caused and continually reinforced by one's own "history". You cannot make a person change no matter how much you would want to do so, but you can try and help create an "emotional environment" that may help a person to *want* to look at change. Seen in this light, this healing mantra can contribute to creating that environment.

This practice is also intended to help you focus on your own feelings, "if I had only paid more attention I would have seen this coming", "I should never have said . . . ", "if I had only visited her more often I could have helped her through her loneliness", etc. All those "if only's" may or may not be realistic, but they are common experiences for care givers and others, and they are sometimes difficult to dispel. Use this healing practice to forgive *yourself* for not being perfect! This helps to "gentle" your mind which in turn can be a powerful contribution to increasing the other person's self-acceptance, reducing guilt feelings, and becoming an invitation to make changes. It is the very opposite of making a person feel guilty or stupid.

* * *

Contemplation.

The purpose of meditation is to relax body and mind, calm down the random thoughts flying uninvitedly through your head, and find a measure of peace and relaxation. But that is the beginning, intended to make space for contemplation.

Contemplation comes from the Latin root templum - a space marked off or designated as a temple: a space set aside for religion and worship. Contemplation indicates using a mental space for objective respectful observation. The term 'objective' means observing an object, thought, or emotion free of judgment - just as it is. This leads to gaining understanding of, and insight into the true nature of the object, thought or emotion.

This definition is almost completely self-explanatory, In order to fully comprehend an object, thought, or emotion, it is necessary to be fully aware of all its properties, its appearance, shape, texture, dimensions, and how it works:

- how it is described,
- how it arrived at its present location,
- its components,
- its environment,
- all values and judgments that are attached to it,
- how a change in the object would change the larger whole,
- how long the object will last without changing.

The purpose of this exercise is not to "investigate" the object; it is simply to observe each aspect and take note of what you observe.

Contemplation is not something that you "do". I often describe contemplation as a state of calm and expectant waiting. When you just sit there, not worrying about whether you forgot to feed the cat etc., you will find that images and impressions enter from your subconscious mind into your awareness (or did those messages come from your guardian angel?). If you can avoid investigating or judging those "messages", you will find that they indeed are trying to tell you something. Much of the content of this book stems from those impressions.

You may have noticed that one aspect is missing: the value of contemplation. This aspect is omitted on purpose because when one adds a value judgment to the contemplation process, one is no longer able to objectively comprehend the object or thought.

Instead, through contemplation one becomes able to observe as if from a distance. It is simply "just there" and "just as it is" with no judgments and no associations attached to it. This way one may learn the true nature of the object, thought, or feeling in its naked reality, and rob it of any power it may have over you because of your own associations with it, or because of the values you, your culture, education, or religion may have attached to it and that you thereby may have adopted.

Please remember that the poplar understanding of contemplation as a way of investigating the value and usefulness of an object is not in line with the true meaning of contemplation. In real contemplation you *do* nothing . . !

What is the purpose of all this hard "doing nothing"? After a while you will begin to notice some subconscious habits that you never even paid any attention to. Take this awareness and make it the focus of your contemplation, and you may be amazed at how powerful these subconscious habits can be, how they control your life, your actions, and your responses to other people and circumstances.

Let's try an simple example. Let's assume that your partner often makes very dark toast for you for breakfast. You don't like dark toast, so one morning you burst out "you always burn the toast and you never listen to me when I ask you not to burn it!" You probably feel powerful and relieved to get it off your chest. You feel right, your partner just seems to ignore you, and you feel justified to set him/her straight once and for all. But what is really happening?

Try and take some contemplative distance from the event. You may begin to notice that:

1. you feel angry; not a good mood to be in for achieving positive change

2. Check for generalizations, 'always' and 'never' are pretty extreme words, powerful when you are angry, but usually less than the truth.

3. The use of the term "you" indicates that you have focused entirely on the other person. Remember that the only person you can change is yourself. The use of "you" is verbal finger pointing and less than effective for achieving change,

4. Is it worth it to start a fight over a piece of toast?

5. Is that toast really burnt or is it just quite dark. Did you use that word "burnt" to make your statement more powerful, to hurt your partner's feelings?

6. Have you checked the toaster? Perhaps it is full of a 2 year supply of bread crumbs that block the timer from working properly. Have you considered cleaning it out?

7. Consider making your own toast. Put 2 slices of bread in the toaster, set the darkness the way you

like it, and push the handle down. Pretty simple! If the result is too dark or too light, experiment a bit till you have it right.

8. Then ask your partner, "when you make toast could you please set the darkness to number 3. (notice the magic word 'please')

9. Is toast the only issue between you and you partner, or is this the tip of an iceberg? Are there other topics you need to talk about in a respectful manner? Can you resolve your anger and then take the initiative to sit down with your partner and start a compassionate conversation for the purpose resolving the issue? (not to win!)

This is a pretty simple example of how contemplation works. Look at the topic dispassionately, see what it consists of, and remedy anything that doesn't seem right. If your pent-up anger gets in your way, deal with that first and separately from the topic, and then try contemplation again. The toast issue is of course pretty contrived but nevertheless a valid example. In other situations there will be other steps in the process of detaching yourself from your anger and from the situation. Please choose a topic from your real life and use it to practise the process.

Notice that you are making changes in yourself and not in your partner, other than asking (politely) to make a change. Now you can begin to become the person you really would like to be. It may or may not turn out to be the beginning of a return to complete health but, whatever your circumstances, it will make your life worthwhile and peaceful.

* * *

Appendix B:

Why Did The Great Whale Breach The Surface ?

As I was waiting in an office, I idly leafed through a magazine and saw a picture of a great whale coming straight up out of the water, more than half its body in the air. Why did that great whale breach the surface?

Frankly, I have no idea, but I have some thoughts on the matter that I want to share with you. First of all, from a practical perspective, what a waste of energy to lift several tons of blubber out of its natural environment for no reason at all, only to come down in 1 or 2 seconds with a bone-shaking crash. . . How useless!

But perhaps there is a secret behind this uselessness. If the whale breached, let's say, to avoid a predator, I can at least feel sorry for the beast. Or let's say the whale did it to lose weight! Hey, what a novel idea! Or maybe just for exercise? Well, at least I found some reasons, but how pedestrian, how useless to occupy my mind with trying to explain something beautiful. So why did the whale breach?

Today, over supper, I listened to a recording of the Dvorak A major violin concerto, a wonderful romantic piece of music. The soloist played it note-perfect, everything was right and every note in its place - and it sounded dead. This truly inspired piece of romantic music soars, in it you can cry, and rage, and swear, and love, and laugh, and soar above the highest clouds. But the soloist played through it without experiencing any of that, and that great piece of beauty and experience ground on for half an hour without ever getting off the ground.

. . . Why did the great whale breach? My fantasy is that she (or he, who knows?) did want to get off the ground or, to be more exact, "break through the surface". Perhaps the whale breached just because it felt like it - or because it was too full of vitality to just stay down there - or because it needed to soar - or because it wanted, however briefly, to have a glimpse of another reality!

Try and explain that? No thank you; I'd rather just live it and experience it and feel it, even at the price of someone commenting "what a waste of energy - how useless".

Life is not a process of finding explanations so we can correctly file our experiences and classify our environment. That is only a function of our paper-thin veneer of intellectual thinking. Underneath that veneer is life itself, to be lived, to be felt, to be experienced, however briefly, for its own life-giving sake.

Life is, and must be, passion. Without passion it is dead no matter how long it lasts. With it, life lasts forever no matter how short it is.

* * *

Appendix C:

Give yourself away.

I almost always pose the following question to people who are living with cancer: "let's assume for a moment that six months from now you are again in perfect health. "What is it that you have learned; what is it that you can give back to life?"

There are two reasons for this question, the first one is to prevent a person from sliding back into his/her habitual "old" lifestyle of false entitlement and emphasis on "I". The second reason is to open the door to a sense of, and participating in, community. Consider doing some volunteer work, whether coaching a sport for kids, volunteering at a community centre or community service program, volunteering as an aid in your child's school, taking a handicapped child out for an activity, visiting an elderly shut-in person, or whatever you are interested in. "Give yourself away" is the motto, and those who are willing and able to do that will feel uplifted and blessed with a spirit-set that is difficult to describe but very real.

And it will most certainly maintain and improve your health.

* * *

Appendix D:

Quotations and Sources.

". . . **there is evidence** of an 'umbilical affect exchange' which influences the . . . immediate and long- term psychology of behaviour. . ." [30]

". . . the unique symbiotic relationship between a mother and her fetus is explored, where issues such as maternal stress and the development of later psychopathology in the child are considered . . ." [31] [32] [33]

" . . .the information associated with . . . trauma is encoded at the cellular level. . . and unless decoded, that cellular memory can serve as the nucleus for psychological and/or psychosomatic illness. . .
. . . various types of meditation, guided imagery, and other mind-body techniques are showing tremendous promise in helping individuals create effective coping mechanisms." [34]

"A study of twins in California last year suggested that experiences in the womb and first year of life can have a major impact". "Studies of animals, for example, have shown that when a rat experiences stress during pregnancy, it can cause epigenetic changes in the fetus that lead to behavioural problems as the rodent grows up". "The good news is that some of these [epigenetic changes], unlike DNA sequences, can be altered. Genes muted by methylation, for example, sometimes can be switched back on again easily". " " . . . Mother Nature writes some things in pencil and some things in pen. . . Things written in pen you can't change. That's DNA. But things written in pencil you can. That's epigenetic". [35]

* * *

Appendix E:

Legislative Authority to Control Job Exports.

The phrase "peace, order and "good govern-ment" describes the principles upon which Canada's Confederation took place. It defines the princi-ples under which the Canadian government should introduce and pass legislation. In section 91 of the Confederation Act, the following phrase describes the legal grounds upon which the federal govern-ment is constitutionally permitted to do so. [36]

POWERS OF THE PARLIAMENT

Legislative Authority of Parliament of Canada .

It shall be lawful for the Queen, by and with the Advice and Consent of the Senate and House of Commons, to make Laws for the Peace, Order, and good Government of Canada, in relation to all Matters not coming within the Classes of Subjects by this Act assigned exclusively to the Legislatures of the Provinces; and for greater Certainty, but not so as to restrict the Generality of the foregoing Terms of this Section, **it is hereby declared that (not-withstanding anything in this Act) the exclusive Legislative Authority of the Parliament of Canada** extends to all Matters coming within the Classes of Subjects next hereinafter enumerated; that is to say,

1.   Repealed.
1A. The Public Debt and Property
2.   **The Regulation of Trade and Commerce.**

. . . followed by several other items to a total of 29

* * *

Appendix F:

A Healing Mantra.

Ho´oponopono is an ancient Hawaiian healing practice of reconciliation and forgiveness that has been practised for many centuries in Hawaii and other Pacific islands for the healing of family strife and criminal behaviour.

More recently, Dr. Ihaleakala Hew Len, who worked as a psychiatrist at the Hawaii State Hospital in the ward for the criminally insane, never saw his patients. He "simply" kept repeating the mantra in order to heal himself, and thereby heal his patients. He believed that every human being, by his or her emotions, thoughts, and behaviours, is connected to the emotions, thoughts, and actions of everyone else, and that honouring that connection to all can affect healing. His experiences in his work have born this out as many of his incurable patients were indeed cured of their extremely serious mental illnesses.

* * *

This may sound very idealistic and unreal: why should I apologize for someone else's wrongdoings? Why should I say "I'm sorry" for another person's mistakes or bad behaviour?

Before we reject this approach let's take a closer look at it. Let's assume that I have a neighbour who doesn't give a hoot about the environment. Instead of recycling, everything goes into the garbage: plastics, metal cans, glass, and more. And he dumps his used motor oil in his backyard, and even burns his old car tires in the yard. This man is really a hazard to our fragile environment. Right?!

Few would disagree with this conclusion. But just a minute, there is more to it than that, My judgment of this man's actions may be justifiable but realize also that I have created a barrier between myself and my neighbour. My judgment in fact states that :"I am right and he is wrong. I am really careful about recycling but he doesn't care; polarity has entered the picture and any meaningful communications between him and me are pretty well shut down. I am right, he is wrong, and until he changes his ways and start to recycle everything, I have no use for this guy.

Now: remember that the only person one can change is oneself, and attempting to change someone else is futile: I can attempt to *force* the other person to change but that may only be temporary and it certainly will create resentment on his part; not a good solution. So what can I do about this situation? If the only person I can change is myself, how can changing myself change his polluting behaviours?

The answer can be found in the following equation: if his behaviour makes me angry (which creates a negative polarizing behaviour in me), my anger is the only thing I can change.

But hey, I am right after all so why should *I* have to change? Don't I have a right, even a duty, to be angry at him!

Really? Then where does that "right to be angry" leave me? Angry, righteous, and ineffective in addressing my neighbour's behaviour. Is that really the kind of person I would like to be? Instead, if I really would like to see my neighbour change his ways, why not address my own anger so that I can at least communicate with him. Here is where the Ho´oponopono healing mantra comes in:

1. I want to neutralize my anger so that I can com-municate with my neighbour in a meaningful way. *"I am sorry"* - about getting angry and judg-mental about him. No need to say this out loud to him; just keep saying it to yourself till you feel more relaxed and less angry.

2. If I really feel uncomfortable or ashamed about my polarizing anger, perhaps I should apologize for that; again, not to my neighbour, but to myself: *"Please forgive me"*.

3. In my mind: If this is all true for me, I need to dispel any and all negative feelings in myself and toward my neighbour. Remember that this refers to *my* feelings, not to my neighbour's actions. To help with that, say *"I love you"*, to myself, and again, not to my neighbour.

4. In short: "neutralize" my own negative feelings and emotions, and my counterpart will sense very soon that I am not judging him, and will feel more free to accept my support and suggestions.

Now, perhaps on a hot summer afternoon, I may want to lean over the fence and invite him over for a cold one on the deck .

* * *

References.

[1] Plato called Athena "the mind of god": a powerful thought taking physical form.

[2] Pablo Neruda, *Bread-Poetry*, The Poetry of Pablo Neruda, p. 674; Farrar, Straus &Giroux, 2003

[3] Individuation: *Man and his Symbols,* C. G. Jung, page 160-161, Dell Publishing Company, New York, 1964

[4] H.H. the Dalai Lama: *How to see yourself as you really are*. p. 49 ff. New York, Atria Books/Simon & Schuster, 2006

[5] http,//en.wikipedia.org/wiki/Life and refer to http,//creativecommons.org/licenses/by-sa/3.0/

[6] http.//en.wikipedia.org/wiki/Life

[7] Neil Turok, PhD, *The Universe within,*. The CBC Massey Lectures, 2012.

[8] Emma Heathcote-James, *They walk among us/ John Blake Publishing Ltd. 2007 ISBN 978-84454-373-1*

[9] Brian L.Weiss, MD. *Many Lives, Many Masters*, Simon & Schuster, 1988

[10] See *www.plumvillage.org* for more details

[11] Institute of Integral Studies in San Francisco. (formerly the California Institute of Asian Studies) http://www.ciis.edu/Academics/Faculty/

[12] cf. *Human life begins on the far end of despair*, Jean-Paul Sartre, *The Flies*

[13] Parabola Magazine, Volume 34, No.1,

". . . life has a purpose and everyone [is] born to go on a kind of quest to find that meaning."

[14] Sircar, Rina. *The Psycho-Ethical Aspects of Abhidhamma* (the advanced teachings of the Buddha), University Press of America, 1999. p. 78, 80.:

[15] http,//en.wikipedia.org/wiki/Spirituality and refer to http,//creativecommons.org/licenses/by-sa/3.0/

[16] http,//en.wikipedia.org/wiki/Spirituality

[17] http,//en.wikipedia.org/wiki/God and refer to http,//creativecommons.org/licenses/by-sa/3.0/

[18] *"God and the Philosophers"* in Honderick, Ted. (ed) *The Oxford Companion to Philosophy, Ted Honderich,* Oxford University Press, 1995

[19] Vergote, Antoine *Religion, belief, and unbelief, a psychological study,* Leuven University Press,1997. p.89

[20] Thanissaro Bhikku *(2004).* (in translated from Pali into English. *Access To Insight. "Both formerly and now, monks, I declare only stress and the cessation of stress.*

[21] Thera, Nyanaponika.. *The Vision of the Dhamma.* Kandy, Sri Lanka, Buddhist Publications Society

[22] Bhikku Bodhi *(2007). "III.1, III.2, III.5".* In Access To Insight. *The All Embracing Net of Views*, Brahmajal Sutta. Kandy, Sri Lanka, Buddhist Publication Society. SEE 40

[23] Thera, Nyanaponika. . *The Vision of the Dhamma.* Kandy, Sri Lanka Buddhist Publications Society

[24] Bhikku, Thannisaro. *The Meaning of the Buddha's Awakening*, Access to Insight 2010

[25] cf. http://www.sonoma.edu/users/d/daniels/jung-sum.html

[26] http://www.studymode.com.essays/2005/07/*do-corporations-have-a-social-responsibility-beyond-stockholder-value-becker*.html

[27] http://www.becker-posner-blog.com/2005/07/*do-corporations-have-a-social-responsibility-beyond-stockholder-value-becke*r.html

[28] Piero Ferrucci. *Inevitable Grace.* Los Angeles, Jeremy Tarcher, 1990

[29] For those interested in pursuing the "meaning" ofd this mantra, visit http:"//www.dharma-haven. org/Tibetan/meaning-of-om-mani-padme-hung. html

[30] Fedor-Freybergh and Vogel, *Encounter with the Unborn, Philosophical Impetus behind Prenatal and Perinatal Psychology and Medicine,*

[31] A.J.Ward, *Prenatal stress and childhood psychopathology.* Child Psychiatry and Human Development 22 (1991, 97-110)

[32] *Decoding traumatic Memory Patterns at the Cellular Level.* Thomas R McClaskey, D.C., C.H.T., B.C.E.T.S.

[33] *National Geographic,* January 2012, p. 64, 65.

[34] Decoding Traumatic Memory Patterns at the Cellular Level. Thomas R. McClaskey, D.C., C.H.T.

[35] *National Geographic,* January 2012, p. 64, 65.

[36] *The Canadian Constitution Act, 1867*

Made in the USA
Charleston, SC
24 February 2015